LÓRÁND HEGYI

NARRATIVES IN CONTEMPORARY ART

Five Essays

SilvanaEditoriale

CONTENTS

NARRATIVES OF THE MULTIPLICITY OF RESPONSIBILITIES

Introduction

"The decline, perhaps the ruin of the universal idea can free thought and life from totalizing obsessions. The multiplicity of responsibilities, and their independence (their incompatibility), oblige and will oblige those who take on those responsibilities, small or great, to be flexible, tolerant, and svelte."
(Jean-François Lyotard, *The Tomb of the Intellectual*, 1984)

In his provocative, radical and irritatingly astute essay *The Tomb of the Intellectual*, Jean-François Lyotard analyzes how the role of "intellectuals" has changed in the course of time; intellectuals situate themselves "in the position of man, humanity, the nation, the people, the proletariat, the creature, or some such entity. They identify with a subject endowed with a universal value. [...] The responsibility of 'intellectuals' cannot be separated from the (generally shared) idea of a universal subject."[1] It is the profound and irreversible crisis facing this universal subject, however, that characterizes our era. As Lyotard puts it: "It is precisely this totalizing unity, this universality, that thought has lacked since at least the middle of the twentieth century."[2]

The social, political and scientific organization of this universal subject, the "totalizing unity" of its history, its development and its objective were reified in "grand narratives" – in the name of a *sensus communis* having universal and collective legitimacy. In his famous book *The Postmodern Condition*, Lyotard postulates that "the grand narrative has lost its credibility, regardless of what mode of unification it uses, regardless of whether it is a speculative narrative or a narrative of emancipation."[3] "Speculative narrative" refers to the rationalistic and scientific explanation of life and of history, while the "narrative of emancipation" alludes to various political strategies aimed at achieving equality, freedom and equilibrium. Both are, in essence, generally valid and attempt to explain the homogenizing totality of life and its developments.

When he speaks of the decline of the unifying and legitimizing power of grand speculative narratives and grand narratives of emancipation, Lyotard identifies the crux of modernity, i.e. the proclivity towards unifying, homogenizing and rationalistically generalizing the complexity of life, towards "a totalizing unity or universality."[4] The crisis of universality, the perception and acceptance of each singular, contextual reality, and empathy for anthropological, situational concreteness all delegitimize the unifying "grand narratives." This causes destabilization, despair and criticism of universal validities and abstract concepts of development, and delegitimizes the rigid, monolithic and intellectual strategies that are incapable of reflecting the concreteness of each specific, historical situation that is ethno-culturally and linguistically determined, and contextually configured. As Michael Newman puts it, the concrete "specific contextual or situational meanings"[5] convey authentic reflections, and these meanings shape the various artistic strategies for exploring *small realities* and immediate, micro-communal situations. The "specific, contextual or situational meanings" convey the concrete realities, value systems, communication models and rules of behavior that have emerged in specific socio-cultural situations and clash with abstract generalizations.

In narratives shaped by contextual and situational realities and concreteness, specific, contextual meanings of intimacy and fragility, personal histories and the singularity of each concrete situation are embodied – the relevant multiplicity of identities and responsibilities, of immanent, situational relations that make no claim to universality, nor to generalizing – and totalizing – homogeneity. On the contrary, such concrete, individual and sensitive structures are capable of perceiving *small realities* without dissipating them in compulsive, totalizing homogenization or negating their contextual idiosyncrasy. The radical concreteness of situational realities and contextual relations delegitimizes any attempt to make abstract, universally valid relevance absolute. The powerful, poetic effectiveness of the concreteness of singular, situational and contextual realities suffuses authentic narration.

Thus emerges a new artistic situation, in which – without any abstract, transcendental or universalistic legitimization – contextual, situational *micro-narratives* directly reflect concrete, micro-communal situations and *small realities* that are intimate, local, personal, and cannot be generalized, operating with empathy and through participation in real, concrete and situational constellations. This enhances sensitivity to concrete diversities, anthropological multiplicity, and the singularity of lived realities. The "concreteness of concrete selves in their immediate societies"[6] described by Arthur C. Danto becomes the core of the new narration of our era's "speaking artists."

Walter Reese-Schäfer, in his analysis of Lyotard, describes this new, modest, down-to-earth responsibility and concreteness that respond without asserting any universalistic claim, grasping and conveying immediate realities without ideology, theology, or the mythology of any theory of salvation. Lyotard's work "The Tomb of the Intellectual" provides intellectuals with new strategies so that they can demonstrate their political commitment without any universalistic legitimizations in the real, non-generalized immediacy of individual situations not assessed by extraneous value systems. "This is what I would like to call a 'new modesty,'" says Walter Reese-Schäfer. "Rather than a totalitarian universalism, Lyotard imagines a kind of 'new responsibility' which expects the collapse of universality and thus perceives the mutual independence, and even the mutual incompatibility, of various responsibilities with flexibility, tolerance, and 'agility,' as the case may be."[7]

Lyotard's "multiplicity of responsibilities," as well as Arthur C. Danto's "multiplicity of our identities and what differentiates us as real,"[8] refer to the re-specification of the subject that no longer represents the object of *grand narratives* as a universal subject, but is understood as a concrete, real, multifariously determined subject of *small realities*. The latter are no longer narratives of "intellectuals," but of artists who operate in specific, distinct, immediate and micro-communal situations and who operate with "local statements."

Viewed from this angle, today's artists are no longer "intellectuals" who might act in the name of universal subjects. Without resorting to lies, messianism, or self-deceit, they can no longer afford to act as the representatives of an absolutized, universal subject. Their competence lies elsewhere – acting in concrete, real and micro-communal situations, exploring specific details, perceiving the particularities of given anthropological constellations, and developing new connections and perspectives through empathy and engagement.

"There seem to be no more 'intellectuals,' and if there are still some left, it is because they are ignorant of what is now a new fact in the history of the Occident (as opposed to the 18th century): there is no universal subject-victim appearing in reality, in whose name thought could draw up an indictment that would be at the same time a 'conception of the world' [...]. The decline, perhaps the ruin of the universal idea can free thought and life from totalizing obsessions. The multiplicity of responsibilities, and their independence (their incompatibility), oblige and will oblige those who take on those responsibilities, small or great, to be flexible, tolerant, and svelte. These qualities are no longer seen as the opposite of rigor, sincerity, and power but as their hallmark."[9]

Naturally, Lyotard's analysis pertaining to the disappearance of the universal subject and the decline of the idea of universality contains just as many aesthetic as ethical and political consequences. When he uses terms such as "flexible," "tolerant," and "svelte," he extends his radical claims to the realm of aesthetics. Adjectives like "flexible" and "svelte," in particular, conjure up a distinctly anti-formalistic, anti-hierarchic, anti-reductivist and anthropological orientation. Immediate reactions, *in situ* actions, the "multiplicity of responsibilities" – they all open up the path towards an aesthetic legitimization of *micro-narratives*. It is the disappearance of universality and the decline of the universal subject that pave the way towards the aesthetic legitimization of *micro-narratives*. The exploration of concrete, micro-communal situations determined by unique and specific conditions disqualifies aesthetic models that are abstract, ahistorical, universalistic, pedagogical and teleological.

Arthur C. Danto, similarly to Lyotard, writes about the importance of concrete, real, micro-communal realities, and about the disappearance of the universal, necessarily abstract, ahistorical subject detached from concrete micro-situations: "A self is not an abstract point of pure reason, the same in all times and climes and cultures. The self, rather, is the concrete product of many forces and causes, which mark it totally. It is in particular the embodiment of its culture, its gender, its traditions, its race [...]. And so an adequate theory of morality must take into account the concreteness of concrete selves in their immediate societies."[10]

Both philosophers speak of the disappearance of the universal, abstract, ahistorical, and de-contextualized subject – which has emerged outside concrete, anthropological, micro-cultural, local, singular and immediate constellations – and of the inextricably linked *obsession* of totality, generalization and homogenization. They both also emphasize the importance of the concreteness of specific, situational and contextual structures of meaning within anthropological, socio-cultural, mental and political constellations, which ultimately determine the poetic coherence of the entirety of fictional and imaginary, visual realities. It is just this new concreteness that makes it possible to perceive the irreducible multiplicity of anthropological realities, without subordinating this vital variety to a single, exclusive, abstract and universal relevance.

The radical rejection of any form of universalistic generalization of the multiplicity of real, concrete situations and anthropological constellations entails aesthetic and ethical consequences, namely the wish – nay, the duty – of the "speaking artists" of our era to directly manifest the concreteness of contextual realities, to grasp the "concreteness of concrete selves in their immediate societies," and to convey it in their visual and sculptural creations. This heralds the perspective of a new, empathic and radical humanism, in which tolerance and acceptance of anthropological specificities, the sensitive perception of specific singularities, and an understanding of the irreducible multiplicity of situational realities appear directly in the structure of meaning of works of art.

Lyotard's line of reasoning on being "flexible," "tolerant" and "svelte" involves ethical and even political ramifications, while also spawning aesthetic entities. Rather than opting for the "obsession of totality," rather than claiming universally valid and timeless strategies deployed on behalf of the "universal subject," the requirement here is to act within the context of immediate realities and of specific, real, irreplaceable situations. *Micro-narratives* address the cultural, mental and emotional situation after the "demise of grand narratives," after the crisis of grand, universal explanations, when artistic interest is focused on the concreteness of situational, contextual realities, on the singularity of anthropological constellations and relations. The narration of a "speaking artist" unfolds in this realm of vivid, contextual realities that do not consider any totalizing, abstract generalizations as relevant – neither ethically nor aesthetically. The artist's voice is shaped by the radical concreteness of diversities and contextual relations.

The three essays published in this book accompany three exhibitions shown in the past decade in Naples, Palermo and Busan. These thematic exhibitions presented artistic statements that manifest a new, empathic, modest and tolerant attitude, an anti-hierarchical, eclectic and anti-monumental orientation, and a skeptical rejection of monolithic systems, while at the same time signaling the artist's responsibility in an era marked by the radicalization of global conflicts between political systems, religions, ideologies, social and cultural value systems. The escalation of brutality and violence, the radicalization of clashes and conflicts, and the increased repression of sovereign reflection and free expression all force artists to make their alarming words heard.

The artist's responsibility consists precisely in a sovereign, skeptical stance vis-à-vis manipulative, repressive systems that often operate with false simplification and generalization, with a false homogenization of the diverse specificities of situational realities. Against the loud, aggressive noise of repressive systems, artists pitch their sensitive, empathic, poetic and independent voices of sovereign thought.

The more subtle, poetic, authentic and sovereign the artists' voices, the more – paradoxically – they are perceived as "speaking artists." Their voices are imbued with empathy, sensitivity, openness, tolerance and authenticity, making them poetically effective, even cathartic. The more carefully, authentically and sensitively the artist's message reflects the specific, contextual concreteness and situational realities, the more decisively the artist's voice manifests resistance against false simplifications and manipulative homogenizations.

Evoking the specific concreteness of anthropological situations, the voice of the "speaking artist" directly reaches people who can hear, beholders who can see. The concreteness of life and the anthropological experience of micro-constellations are apparent in the artist's voice, which speaks – as Gilbert & George describe so beautifully and passionately – of life, of fundamental, lived experience: "We want Our Art to speak across the barriers of knowledge directly to People about their life and not about their knowledge of art [...]. We want the most accessible form with which to create the most modern speaking visual pictures of our time."[11]

Such art speaks of anthropological realities, of life as it is configured in the infinitely varied realities of each concrete constellation. The "most modern speaking visual pictures of our time" evoked by Gilbert & George refer to a picture's effective message, to the communication of meaning as a fundamental vocation of art, and to the "speaking artist's" anti-formalistic, content-centered, involved and proactive endeavor to create the strongest, most expressive, affecting and effective, visual narrative. Such authentic visual narratives embody anthropological realities with their specific, situational meanings, contradicting any false generalizations or abstract homogenization, and skeptically rejecting any monolithic system. They offer poetic *micro-narratives* that express a personal engagement in immediate realities and sensitive empathy, at the same time redefining the localization of artistic practice in the dense variety of encompassing social processes.

Micro-narratives of the situationally determined, fragile and fleeting specificities of anthropological realities are attempts to redefine artistic practice in the thicket of complex, socio-cultural situations. With a fragmentary, spontaneous and anti-teleological receptiveness that is tolerant, open and sensitive, they reflect the typical post-utopian condition of our current era and propose new, fitting, credible and modest interpretations.

Flexibility, tolerance, agility and empathy are elements contained in a new strategy of *poetic modesty* with which immediate *small realities* are perceived and assessed. This particular aspect seems to be of profound significance for contemporary artistic practice: it is these very artists who place nuances and intimacies, immediate realities and sensitive details at the center of their work, thereby greatly enhancing *empathy*.

Empathy and poetic openness towards fragile, anthropological constellations, a natural and intimate articulation of *small realities*, an interest taken in the contextual, situational and immediate systems of meaning of *micro-communities*, an empathic perception of situational meanings and idiosyncrasies, and a state of submersion in a diverse, concrete, distinct *micro-cultural density* characterized by specific entities and constellations, and impossible to generalize – these seem to be the salient features of such authentic narratives, such *micro-narratives*. Dreams and mental projections, personally experienced and culturally learned situations, immediate *small realities*, and the socio-cultural simulacrum become mingled in such a sensitive *micro-narrative*. "Situational meanings," rather than universal, abstract, transcendental and external meta-levels, shape their immanent, socio-cultural relationality.

In contemporary artistic practice, a quiet, gentle and modest refusal of any concept of transcendental universality and of all forms of "common reason" seems to be taking hold. Artists now reaffirm their engagement in immediate realities and their perception of diversity as their primary attitude and reflected position. "This involves an emphasis on the specific contextual or situational meaning of the elements and the work of art which moves in the opposite direction to Lévi-Strauss' sublation of particular elements of myth into a universal combinatory," writes Michael Newman.[12] Hence, various, specific messages, communications and references may not be able to boast any external and general legitimizing systems applied outside the bounds of immediate and real situations; rather, they are conditioned by concrete contexts. Instead of transcendental universality, meaning is shaped by *immanent relationality.* Michael Newman's "specific contextual or situational meaning" is foregrounded as a pertinent basis for contemporary artistic work. Contextual and situational meaning makes no claim to universal and abstract validity – on the contrary, it alludes to immediate, contextual realities. It reflects specific ethno-cultural, historical and traditional realities, as well as economic and geopolitical conditions, and circumstances of intellectual history; language, education, sexuality, communication, myths and religion, as well as our relationships to nature, bodies, the past, memory and utopia, determine this *immanent relationality*.

Re-contextualizing artistic practice in complex, contradictory, cultural and historical processes, the varied inclusion of diverse, micro-cultural and communal references, the activation and invigoration of metaphorical, allegorical and contextual, semiotic systems localize the work of contemporary artists in modest, immediate *small realities*, in which cultural metaphors function only as limited, relative suggestions of certain forms of pathos stripped of monumentality. These *small realities* do not aspire to universal legitimization; instead, they refer to immediate, anthropological constellations, to micro-cultural, micro-communal and situational meanings, and the intensity of their emotional, poetic and metaphorical suggestions shapes the specific, artistic effectiveness of such narratives.

In this respect, one of Lyotard's arguments is especially interesting and significant. In the following passage, he distinguishes between the vocation of the artist and the function of the "intellectual": "An artist, a writer, a philosopher only needs to answer the question, What is painting, writing, thought? If you tell him, Your work is incomprehensible to most people, he has the right and the duty to ignore this objection. His addressee is not the public, not even the 'community' of artists, writers, etc. In truth he does not know who his addressee is, and this is precisely what it means to be an artist, a writer – to send out your 'message' into the desert."[13] This message does not refer to any idealized and adulterated, universal subject on whose behalf the "intellectual" once spoke. Rather, it refers to the specific and distinct micro-communal situations of *small narratives*, which unfold within a "multiplicity of responsibilities" or a "multiplicity of our identities."

This new, empathic and sensitive art of relative and limited relevance is the art of skeptical artists who have renounced all attempts at universal legitimacy, not of "intellectuals" who operate on behalf of a fictional, universalistic and utopian authority. Its pathos, and at the same time its "normalcy," resides in the recognition of the limited and relative power of universalistic explanations and ethical value systems. This art is gentle, intimate, relativistic, sensitive and empathic, but at the same time also subversive, skeptical and provocative, anarchic, anti-hierarchical and anti-monumental. Its intelligence, poetic effectiveness, and subversive, liberating power draw upon the radical concreteness of contextual constellations, a multiplicity of responsibilities and identities, immanent relationality – not upon external, hierarchical, mythical or ideological legitimization. Its intelligence manifests in its empathic capacity to establish new connections. That is why Lyotard's beautiful and modest words seem particularly apt to close this essay: "Intelligences do not fall silent, they do not withdraw into their beloved work, they try to live up to this new responsibility which renders the 'intellectuals' troublesome, impossible: the responsibility to distinguish intelligence from paranoia..."[14]

1. Jean-François Lyotard: *Grabmal des Intellektuellen*, Edition Passagen, Vienna 1985, p. 10.
2. Ibid., p. 16.
3. Jean-François Lyotard: *Das postmoderne Wissen*, Edition Passagen, Vienna 1994, p. 112.
4. Ibid., p. 113.
5. Michael Newman: *Revising Modernism, Representing Postmodernism.*
6. Arthur C. Danto: *Philosophizing Art*, University of California Press, Berkeley-Los Angeles-London 1999, pp. 124-125.
7. Walter Reese-Schäfer: *Lyotard zur Einführung*, Junius Verlag, Hamburg 1988, p. 54.
8. Arthur C. Danto: "Postmodern Art and Concrete Selves. The Model of the Jewish Museum," in: Arthur C. Danto, op. cit., pp. 124-125.
9. Jean-François Lyotard: *Grabmal des Intellektuellen*, op. cit., p. 17.
10. Arthur C. Danto: "Postmodern Art and Concrete Selves. The Model of the Jewish Museum", in: Arthur C. Danto, op. cit., pp. 124-125.
11. Gilbert & George.
12. Michael Newman: *Revising Modernism, Representing Postmodernism.*
13. Jean-François Lyotard: *Grabmal des Intellektuellen*, op. cit., p. 13.
14. Jean-François Lyotard: *Grabmal des Intellektuellen*, op. cit., p. 18.

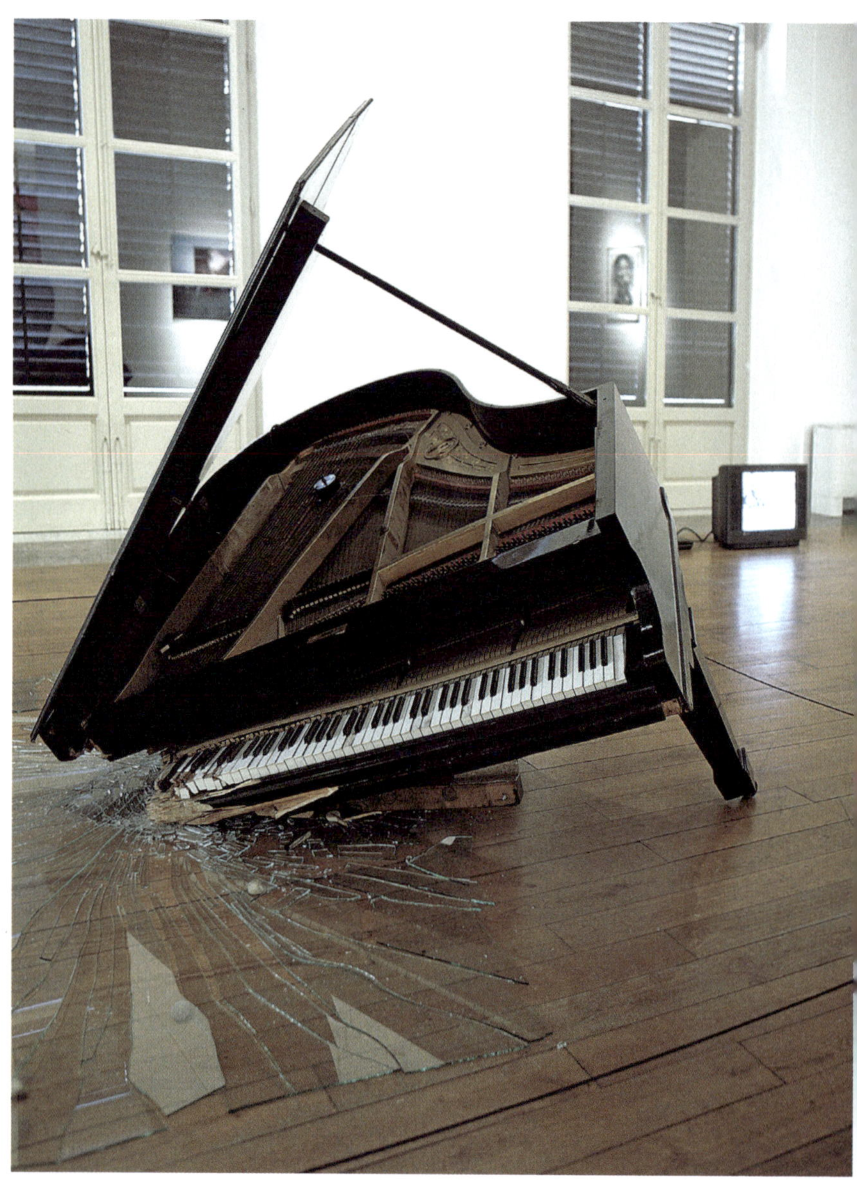

Günther Uecker
Fall, 1988
Piano, glass, electric DVD, variable dimensions
Courtesy of the artist
Photo © Fabio Sgroi

ESSENTIAL EXPERIENCES

Time, Death, Radicality and Responsibility

"Le maintenant, c'est le fait que je suis maître, maître du possible, maître de saisir le possible. La mort n'est jamais maintenant.
Quand la mort est là, je ne suis plus là, non point parce que
que je suis néant, mais parce que je ne suis pas à même de saisir."
(Emmanuel Levinas, *Le temps et l'autre*)

At the end of the time given to man is death, which every living being fears. This fear is as old as man and his myths, his great narratives, his religions, rituals and symbols. Awareness of death means awareness of the finiteness of the time given to man. The perception of time is possible for man through perception of the end of the time given, the absence of time, and therefore through the perception of timelessness. Life exists in time and unfolds in the interval between birth and death. For man, birth and death mean the beginning and the end of the time we are given. This time given to man, to every living being, limited but real and concrete, is the only time that matters to man, that is not an abstraction but real life. For man, life is the possibility of the perception of time, and this implies, paradoxically enough, perception of the tragic finiteness of time.

Humanly relevant time exists for man only through the possibility of the perception of time itself, and this is life. With death, the time given to man is no more. In other words, when the perception of time ceases, so does life. For man, the ceasing of time means death. As Emmanuel Levinas wrote about the relationship between death and time: "This is why death is never a present reality. This is self-evident. The old aphorism designed to dispel the fear of death, namely that where you are, death is not and vice versa, fails utterly and unquestionably to recognize the paradox of death because it ignores our relationship with it, which is a unique relationship with the future. The aphorism does, however, have at least the merit of insisting on the eternal futurity of death. [...] death is *inapprehensible* [...] it marks the end of the subject's manhood and heroism. Nowness is the fact that I have power, power over the possible, power to apprehend the possible. Death is never now. When death is here, I no longer am, not because I am nothingness, but because I am no longer able to apprehend. My mastery, my manhood, my heroism as subject can neither be manhood nor heroism in relation to death. In suffering, where we sense the proximity of death – and still at the phenomenal level – there is this reversal of the activity of the subject into passivity."[1]

The act of apprehension and perception, and hence the possibility of one and the other, is the content of life. This activity of the subject is the essential, fundamental content of life, and its impossibility, namely passivity, is the end of life. Time has no human meaning if it cannot be perceived by man. It has no meaning for life; it is inapprehensible. It is only in the act of perception on the part of man that time taken on human meaning. Without the perceiving subject, the objective time existing outside the human domain is completely irrelevant for mankind and remains a pure abstraction. It will therefore never be possible to transfer the consideration of rigid, abstract, fatalistic time, divorced from human perception and human activity, into any concrete anthropological situation.

The act of the perception of time – through recognition of the finiteness of time – enables us to understand life as time, as a given interval that is useful and usable in the context of the human domain. Awareness of the finiteness of this interval generates anguish because man does not know and cannot truly understand what will come afterwards, because man cannot understand that perception will no longer be possible at all. This harrowing impossibility is the reason for suffering and

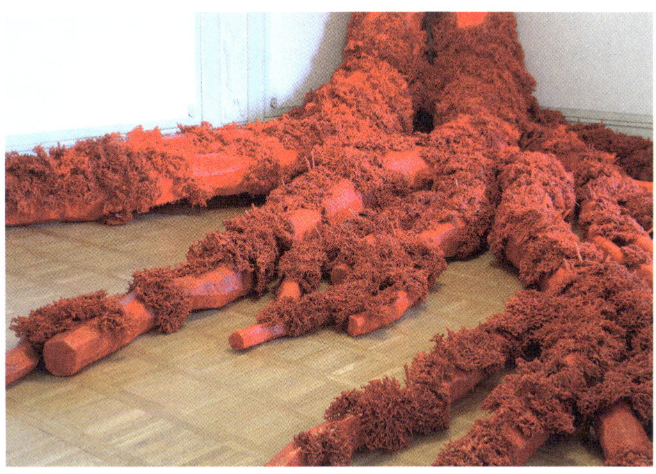

Paolo Grassino
Madre, 2008
Wax on polystyrene and wood, variable dimensions
Courtesy of the artist
Photo © the artist

fear: "The important thing in the approach of death is that at a certain moment *we are no longer able to be able*; and is precisely for this reason that the subject loses his mastery as subject."[2]

The loss of mastery as subject is the tragic, unbearable impossibility of perception and of action at the same time. The possibility of perception and the ability to apprehend manifest the "manhood and heroism of the subject," in other words, "his mastery as subject." This mastery is life; its loss is death. The fear of death – which accompanies the witting or unwitting spirit all the way through life and can completely overwhelm it in certain difficult moments – arises from recognition that there is a state at a certain point in which the subject loses his mastery as subject.

In this context, the loss of mastery as subject means the loss of responsibility. The heroism of the subject is closely related to responsibility: responsibility for time, responsibility for the mastery of the subject in the interval of time given to him, responsibility for the other. The manhood of the subject implies, immediately and inevitably, the ethical aspect of responsibility: responsibility for the time given, the time of activity, the time of perception and apprehension, of responsibility for the other. As Emmanuel Levinas wrote in *Entre nous*: "All men are responsible for one another, and I am more than anyone else [...]. It is the fundamental characteristic of the human being as morally responsible. Responsibility is an individuation, a principle of individuation."[3] It is precisely this responsibility that makes it possible to understand what Levinas means by the heroism of the subject. It is the heroism of the responsible subject. When Levinas says that dying is returning to this state of irresponsibility, to the sobbing of a child, he touches on a delicate and incredibly complex point regarding the intellectual and emotional perception of death, where the utmost tragedy encounters the utmost irony and becomes one with it. This disconcerting and irritating fusion is an essential element of the aesthetic mechanisms, which prompt a radicalization of emotional intensity and, with it, participation on the part of the viewer.

This radicalization of emotional and intellectual intensity constitutes the specific entity of a hypersensitivity that manifests itself in art and regards the essential experiences, understood as the crucial events in our life. Within this context, the perception of time means perception of the time we are given: life and the perception of life as self-fulfillment, as process, as creative energy, as responsibility for the organization and enjoyment of the time we are given, internalization of the essential experiences as the basis of orientation. This fundamental orientation – which decides everything, informs our attitude as a whole, and determines our stance with respect to the most important choices and events – manifests itself in the concentration of the work of art. In the various forms of art, essential experiences are perceived and thematized through materialization in various contexts. The essential experiences become perceptible only in this materialization; they do not exist outside contexts that are human, i.e. real, concrete and anthropological. It is through these various cultural and anthropological contexts that indivisible links are forged between the different spheres and fields of organized human life, the processes of work and learning, the intelligible structures, the languages and semiotic systems, the rites and myths, the great metaphors of humanity.

The exhibition "Essential Experiences" focuses primarily on the processes of temporal perception and their contextualization in cultural metaphors. At one level, with great sensitivity, various perceptual processes presenting both slow, tranquil and almost imperceptible changes and the sudden, dramatic transformations and outbursts of emotion are shown as metaphorical events and hence as metamorphoses of entities endowed with metaphorical significance. At the other level of this confrontation with the artistic perception of time, i.e. with its cultural contextualization, the focus is on the problems of narration and the juxtaposition is between dramaturgical strategies and mechanisms that operate on the one hand through defamiliarization, subversive irony, radical changes of value in the conventional forms of pathos and their legitimization, and express on the other the cogent, cathartic immediacy of participation and emotional involvement.

The slowness or rapidity of the changes – or their perception – is transferred from the physical plane to the metaphorical plane of cultural contextualization. Poetic, calm, stark, simple, subtle and moving, pared down to the monotonous rhythm of the body breathing, Kimsooja's video thus prompts contemplative reflection on time, on the relationship with the body and nature, on the problems of intervention and participation, on the harmony between man and nature, the given and the designed, but also on silent disappearance, on acceptance of the dissolving of life and the passing of time, thereby generating pantheistic coherence and unity. The small, slow, almost imperceptible, monotonously repeated movements of the body lying on a huge round boulder, massive. immutable and immovable, and breathing with a regular rhythm create a very particular sense of time that suggests eternal repetition and the dematerialization of physical things at the same time. The perception and internalization of time in the context of self-awareness also involve the complexity of responsibility for the other, or rather the responsibility of artistic practice that offers exemplary manifestos on the basis of personal experience.

The slowness of the processes of plastic-visual transformation or their perception prompts the beholder to internalize the latent changes as metaphorical processes and relate them to the different cultural contexts. Some artists therefore operate with the extremely slow and possibly long flow of certain processes of restructuring or physical changes – or with their perception – that refer to other, metaphorical levels of meaning. Examples include Roman Opalka, Giuseppe Penone, Richard Nonas, Pedro Cabrita Reis, Lee Ufan and Kimsooja, in whose works the perception of the flow of time is immediately related to metaphorical structures of value encapsulating important characteristics drawn from linguistic systems and the different organizational forms of human life.

There is always something quintessentially metaphorical in the relationship between life and art, between the personality of the artist and his or her work, between aesthetic self-fulfillment and private self-destruction. Art is always a metaphor of life and, at the same time, a strategy adopted to counter its finiteness. Immanent in principle, the world of the artwork is born out of the complexity of the vital processes even when art is understood and created as an autonomous "anti-world" with respect to life. The immanent structures of the image are in principle not those of life and their teleological processes are determined by an ultimate aesthetic end (vision, utopia, "dream"), which exists only in fiction, in uncompromising artistic representation, and towards which the entire production tends constantly and coherently over the years. The viewer experiences this vision on observing the images. It is only in the act of looking that the artist's vision can be reconstructed in the imagination. Metaphorically, reconstruction of the artist's utopia is the intelligible self-fulfillment of the beholder, who attains another dimension of thought through the act of perception and internalization, and thus undergoes change. At the same time, it also means the disappearance of the artist – who has become irrelevant for the purposes of the universal validity of the vision – as a private person. This is an absolutely essential element of responsibility, to which crucial and central importance is attached in the artist's work.

The radicality of the artist is not arbitrary but the fruit of personal responsibility, which makes it necessary to address only the true issues and essential experiences. Roman Opalka's unequalled radicality derives precisely from this responsibility. He cannot allow himself to any degree or in any form to depart arbitrarily from the rigorous logic of his system. He must carry on his project responsibly *ad absurdum*, to the very end.

Artist and viewer move parallel to one another, which endows the element of time with a mystical and extraordinarily "technical" meaning. In Roman Opalka's work, looking at an image always requires a certain length of time, even in the case of a single painting. From the beginning to the end of one of his works, the eye follows not only the row of figures but also the process of their formation, and the formal appearance is identical in this to the passage of time. The act of looking implies reconstruction of the painting's internal structure and the period of time involved in its creation. Looking at a series of paintings is equivalent to reproducing this internalization of the reconstruction of the passage of time. The beholder identifies with the artist; the movement of the eye repeats the movement of the hand. The passing of time thus becomes the fundamental methodological issue in the observation of the painting, which paradoxically gives rise to two different levels of interpretation.

On the one hand, the painting is regarded as the embodiment of a working process, a term to be understood in both an aesthetic and an ethical sense. This titanic work has been performed for decades now with asceticism, self-control, patience and coherence, even though the end result will never be visible as a sensorially comprehensible whole. The gradual disappearance of differences – in the sense of the Suprematist leaning towards abstraction and balance – means the disappearance of form on the sensory surface of the actual painting as a primary aesthetic principle. The white figures painted on the surface of the painting, which is gradually becoming lighter, are approaching a state in which the difference between them and the white background will no longer be optically perceptible. At this point, the aesthetic form will disappear as a sensorially comprehensible and visually defined phenomenon of artistic creation. Roman Opalka sacrifices form in order to formulate the silent, timeless, spiritual metaphor of universal harmony, balance and unity. He jettisons everything that distinguishes one artist from another, what constitutes the richness of an artist.

At the same time, the painting suggests an essence of existence wholly independent of life, of physical, material processes, of human plans, efforts and aspirations, an essence has no links with its origin, the artist's work, temporal human activity and morality. The painting has been detached from the temporal process through which it was formed and undergone self-dissociation in order to manifest the difference in principle between life and art. While this now seems to contradict the thesis formulated above, namely that the painting as working process allows itself to be interpreted through the passing of time, the enigmatic richness of Roman Opalka's work rests basically on this paradox. The painting is both an unfortunately fleeting moment in an eternal process aimed at capturing the truth and essence of existence and a real, physical object that exists outside time, autonomous and spiritual, a complete image of existence. While the first interpretation proceeds through the internalization of life as process and therefore conceals a moral lesson within itself (almost a new metaphor of *vanitas* after the heroic age of the utopianism of the avant-garde movements), the second manifests the anthropological aspect more deeply. In this respect, Opalka creates a metaphor of time that demonstrates the impossibility of perception, and hence the moment after which, as Levinas put it, "we are no longer able to be able."

The material supports of the spatial structure are immediately related in the work of Richard Nonas to an immaterial, intelligible temporal structure, which is thereby connected with decision-making mechanisms and hence anthropological challenges. Even though the apparently simple and transparent physical structure fashioned by the artist contains no anecdotal elements, the slow reconstruction of the overall structure takes shape as a standing challenge to take decisions, to make plans, to follow or reject projections. An authentically dramaturgical situation thus arises whereby the passage of time is made up of a complex system – open but somewhat pressing and labori-

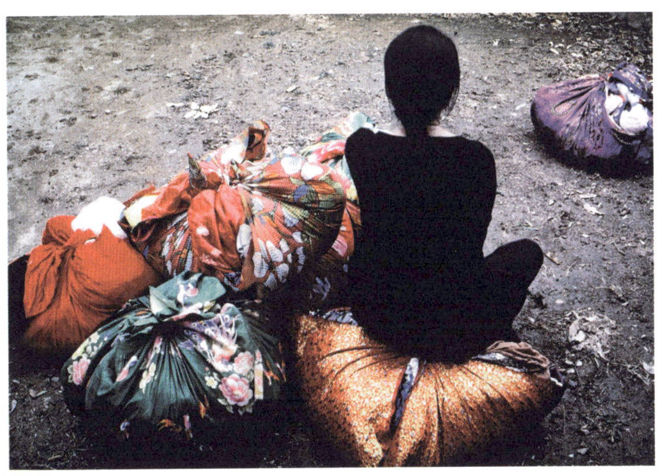

Kimsooja
Cities on the Move - 11633 Mile Bottari Truck Artist with Bottaris, 1997-2001
Duraclear photographic print in light box, unmounted print size 124 x 188.8 cm
Courtesy Kewenig Galerie, Cologne
Photo © Simon Vogel

ous – of decisions and revisions, reconstructions and revisions. The slow perception of the spatial situation – with the details that succeed one another and the relationships between spatial units that, through the precisely calibrated arrangement of similar repeated elements, transform the given space and give visual form to relations, directions of movement, lines of energy, challenges and indications – heightens our awareness of time to the same extent as the slow reconstruction of the indications manifesting themselves prompts on each occasion a plan, a decision-making strategy, the adoption of a stance. Once again, the ethical coherence of Richard Nonas is a manifestation of responsibility with respect to the other, because the constant and consistent strategy of the challenge to take decisions is related in his work to the economy of time, to the perception of time, to the concentration and selection of entities endowed with value.

Lee Ufan endeavors in the same way to find a comprehensive, effective figurative metaphor capable of displaying anthropological realities with no mediation and marking the inevitable contradiction between vital processes and semiotic systems with dramatic and undistanced immediacy. The artist's starting point is the assumption that the work of art cannot and must not be isolated from the stratified mental, socio-cultural and anthropological context moulded by cultural tradition, worldview, the convention of forms of communication and metaphorical structures of signs. The work of art lives within this densely layered context of symbolic forms and conventional semiotic structures, learned and internalized in long temporal processes that underpin our anthropological contextualization and intelligible orientation. This means that the individual work of art is not an allegory, an imitation of something external, but lives in the context of the outside world, of life, of socio-cultural realities, so that the internal structure of the visual-plastic phenomenon receives its meaning obviously and naturally in the anthropological context of our existence. In this sense, the apparent autonomy of the work of art is not to be understood as an allegory of freedom, as long suggested by Greenberg's interpretation, but as a phenomenon of the obvious, immediate language that is born and functions in the dense anthropological, mental and socio-cultural context. Language that can really be described as such is inseparable from the context of its speakers. On this view, there are no rigid, impenetrable boundaries between the autonomous work of art and external realities. It is, however, precisely these external realities – which are external only in appearance and actually constitute the very locus of meetings and connections – that appear in the specific visual-plastic entity of the work of art because they form part of the anthropological complexity of our existence.

This point is particularly important in the case of Lee Ufan, whose art has been always considered Asian in the sense of outside the aesthetic structure of Western discourse. The essential and radical nature of his approach stems from his insertion of Eastern formal conventions into a completely different sphere, namely an anthropological context where so-called "traditional formal language" is not perceived as something that is only aesthetically autonomous but as *anthropologically integrated*, embedded and included in the complex socio-cultural praxis. For this reason, it is essential to consider Lee Ufan's painting within the context of *real anthropological perceptual processes* and not as a mere reinterpretation or slightly banal updating of the Eastern tradition. Even though he naturally comes from this cultural tradition, this is by no means a sufficient reason to consider his creations in terms of this cliché. It is instead important to focus primarily on his immediacy and anthropological rootedness, in which the concentration on the creation of rich, elastic, flexible and *responsive metaphors* is subordinated to the connections between organized forms of life and systems of signs.

Slowness rather than speed, deep silence rather than loud noises, reduction and parsimony rather than the hedonistic accumulation of every possible object, apparently monotonous repetition rather than quick and apparently daring changes in method, respect for space and its limits rather than an assault on space and contempt for boundaries, discreet self-mastery rather than subjectivistic-activistic escalation of the ego: all these elements are related to a hidden, but vitally important and fundamentally substantial ethical plane of artistic practice that unites radicality with responsibility, with man's orientation in terms of principle. The artist's responsibility manifests itself in the radicality of the decision to concentrate on the essential, to forgo personal particularity in this concentration or transfer it to another plane.

Giuseppe Penone works in the same way with the slow perception of temporal processes, empathetically shifting their flow and its consequences to other planes. He displays emotionally effective physical and sensible phenomena that give objective shape to a similarity between intelligible structures and the empirical, physical and sensible natural world. The similarity helps us to reflect on time, change and impermanence, to explore the process of work as effective, productive activity, as fertile, creative employment that also leaves signs in its wake. It helps us to meditate on our role and on what is essential in life, to verify our relationship with nature, with self-organizing, vegetative, primal, physical reality. Each of his works offers different pathways of thought in which evaluation of the natural

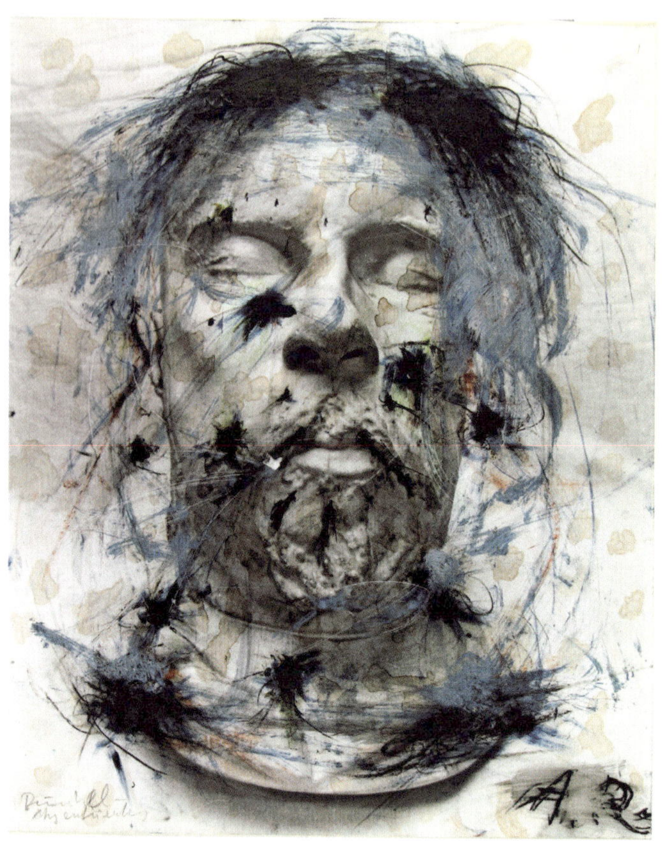

Arnulf Rainer
Totenmaske, end of the 1970s
Mixed media on photo, 60 x 50 cm
Courtesy Heike Curtze Gallery, Vienna

processes of accumulation and the reciprocal artificial/artistic processes – i.e. the processes of reduction – contributes to the internalization of the passage of time as metaphorical change, transformation, metamorphosis. It is precisely this change, this act of transformation, that lies at the centre of his work.

In a well-known work, Penone grafted a bronze cast of his own hand onto the trunk of a young tree so that the rigid and immutable metal object squeezed and pressed against the body of the living and growing plant, thus making visible at various levels the metaphorical, ethical and emotional significance both of the passing of time and of the confrontation between different organized forms of life and their symbolic values. The human hand is one of its most intelligent and able tools of the human body and has, for this very reason, become a symbol of creation and work but also prayer and taken on different meanings in spheres such as politics, religion, power and resistance. Its reproduction and insertion in the natural situation constitute a human intervention in nature that involves both an aesthetic and a metaphorical aim. What has been created here is a demonstration of two different organizational systems. Deliberate human activity, teleologically meditated and systematically executed, is juxtaposed with the natural, vegetative, biological and immediate developmental processes of nature, which know nothing of teleology, nothing of ends or symbols. The bronze object remains unchanged, incapable of adapting to the physical change of the trunk, which slowly grows, develops and becomes stronger. On the contrary, it begins to act as a brake, putting up a stubborn resistance that is ultimately unable to control, restrain or halt the powerful energy of nature, the strength of the tree. The bronze hand slowly disappears. The trunk builds up around and over it to the point where the foreign body is incorporated into the body of the tree. Absorbed forever by the forces of nature, it can no longer be removed. In this simple and at the same time dramatic constellation, different forms of energy, different forces, different intentions or spontaneous processes are presented in vital and powerful juxtaposition, thus giving birth to a poetically effective metaphor that encapsulates great ethical and aesthetic issues.

The above-mentioned hypersensitivity, one of the fundamental elements of artistic activity or the work of art, draws upon the essential experiences of life, which are necessarily perceptible only in the real, concrete time given to man. This element manifests itself with boundless radicality in the dramatic moments of essentiality, moments that are present in all the spheres of life and all the anthropological and cultural fields. Hypersensitivity radicalizes emotionality and creates intense, explosive, challenging, deep, painful and disturbing metaphors in which dramatic juxtapositions of antagonistic forces and intentions in conflict with one another give birth to extremely evocative, strong, aggressive and destructive or often self-destructive formations, displaying almost unbearable concentration on the crucial moment.

The painful immediacy of the dramatic encounter with the intolerable finiteness of the time given to man prompts radical, disturbing, destructive and self-destructive revolts that strive with the radicality of resistance for the impossible: to deny finiteness, understood as the finiteness of time and of responsibility for one's time. As Levinas wrote, "Dying means returning to this state of irresponsibility." This means that death is irresponsibility and life responsibility. For this reason Levinas describes death as *inapprehensible*: "it marks the end of the manhood and heroism of the subject."[5]

This scandalous, unacceptable and unbearable elusiveness is the central content of a series of works presented in this exhibition, which relate to different essential experiences of limiting situations in life. Extreme emotionality, accentuated drama or irony taken to the point of absurdity, subversive and piercing humor all bring the viewer face to face with the crisis of perception, the painful impossibility of apprehension, the condition of irresponsibility that dramatically finds expression in "the approach of death," as Levinas wrote. The heroic resistance against the loss of the responsibility, freedom and heroism of the subject – against capitulation or abdication of the subject's mastery, against the intolerable return to the condition of irresponsibility – creates dramatic or heroic visions by means of radical emotionality or strong, challenging and powerful metaphors of the struggle by means of subversive irony and radical absurdity. Both paths challenge viewers and force them to abandon their neutrality, to get involved in the dramatic processes of the revolt, the battle, the pursuit of mastery, freedom and full responsibility. The radicality of this concentration on the intolerability of irresponsibility, on the never acceptable and on dreadful finiteness, draws once again on responsibility, which essentially moulds the fundamental orientation of the artist.

Dramatic protests against the destruction of man's mastery, against the inexplicable and unforgivable alienation of his freedom, his possibility of perception, his manhood and his heroism permeate the work of Günther Uecker, Jan Fabre, William Kentridge, Michelangelo Pistoletto and Danica Dakic'. The destruction of the piano in Günther Uecker's installation metaphorically represents both the annihilation of a people along with its culture and culture itself. Uecker's work refers to the burning of the books of Jewish authors, the ban on performing the music of Jewish composers, the arbitrary, brutal, fanatical, racist division of cultural creation into "healthy" art and "degenerate" art, Arian and Jewish culture, an act that destroyed the whole of German culture. With the destruction of the piano, music is destroyed, the possibility of creating music and listening to music is abolished, and culture loses its legitimacy. The voice of music is outlawed, replaced with the brutal noises of the piano being smashed into pieces, and brutality reigns alone as the absolute sovereign.

The sad and deeply moving homage paid by Jan Fabre to all the slaughtered innocent, to all the suffering and the fallen, presents massacre as the perverse rite of an unknown, furious, cruel and boundless negativity. The artist harnesses a radicalization of emotionality that works through terrible, invasive and concrete images of our existence to convey the essential experiences verging on the unbearable with no regard for moral taboos, aesthetic conventions or the conventional forms and limits of language. Fabre's radicality is the immediate visibility of his responsibility, which offers us no didactic explanations but confronts us with images full of death and suffering. Both Uecker and Fabre work with the dramatic moment, the compression of time, a focus on the atrocious and appalling moment of definitive destruction.

Revelations of ethically impossible, intolerable and unacceptable conditions – revelations of a strongly emotive, moving, personal and painful character – find expression in the works of William Kentridge, who represents the eternal flight of man, the forced wandering through cities and nations, by land or sea, in the heat or the cold, by day or night, alone or with one's friends and family, or even with contemporary strangers sharing the same refugee status. In his melancholy comments on life and death, the past and memory, personal drama and collective suffering, this great artist and poet speaks about the destiny of millions and millions of people, materializing constant repetition as the experience of time in the context of the historical experiences of modern mankind. Repetition, monotony and slowness are part of a narrative that develops over time and shifts the perception of the slow passing of time onto the metaphorical plane of generalization and the historical materialization of experiences that are simultaneously ancient and present.

Resistance and revolt, uncompromising radicality, the subversive challenging of certain absolute and apparently stable socio-culturally and morally coercive conventions, all these elements manifest themselves in the stage-like installations of Gloria Friedmann, which address the complexity and poetic multiplicity of this contextualization of death, the complex narrative built up around the mythical figure of death in the Western culture. At the heart of this simultaneously picturesque, obscure and tragicomic narrative is opposition, refusal, calling into question the power of death and the authority of the unknown, elusive, invisible, mysterious figure who takes to the decisions and seems to direct events. The general and boundless challenging of all conventional authority and every role in the power game leads to a dramatic and disconcerting destabilization of the world. There is no longer any position that appears certain and legitimate; no responsibility is perceived. No hierarchy, authority or moral judgment appears to be authentic and acceptable because what is seen everywhere is only a theatre of appearance.

This general fatalistic and boundless destabilization of all the possible systems of values, which makes a fundamental orientation absolutely impossible in ethical questions and an ontological context, creates absurd images of an eternal dispute between figures hidden behind masks that play different roles without making their true legitimacy credible. There is no ethical credibility in this theatre of the absurd, where the figure of

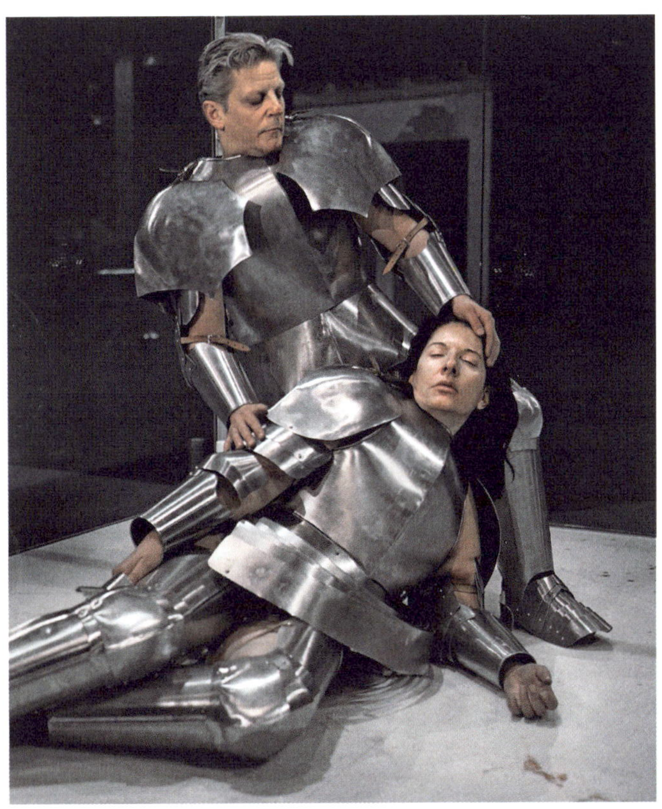

Marina Abramović, Jan Fabre
Virgin Warriors (Pietà), 2006
Color C-print
Courtesy of the artist

death plays a perversely hedonistic game with its victims and develops a dialogue on being and non-being, power and powerlessness, happiness and unhappiness. These questions are, however, only apparently addressed in this dialogue, because the other party is utterly incapable of giving honest answers. The cynical figure of death is the absolute sovereign, dancing and celebrating its power, letting itself be seduced in the arms of a gigolo. There is no true love or true emotion but the perverse, macabre, grotesque world of the appearance of instantaneous pleasure, which diverts our attention from the real questions.
Gloria Friedmann creates a theatre of the absurd where the

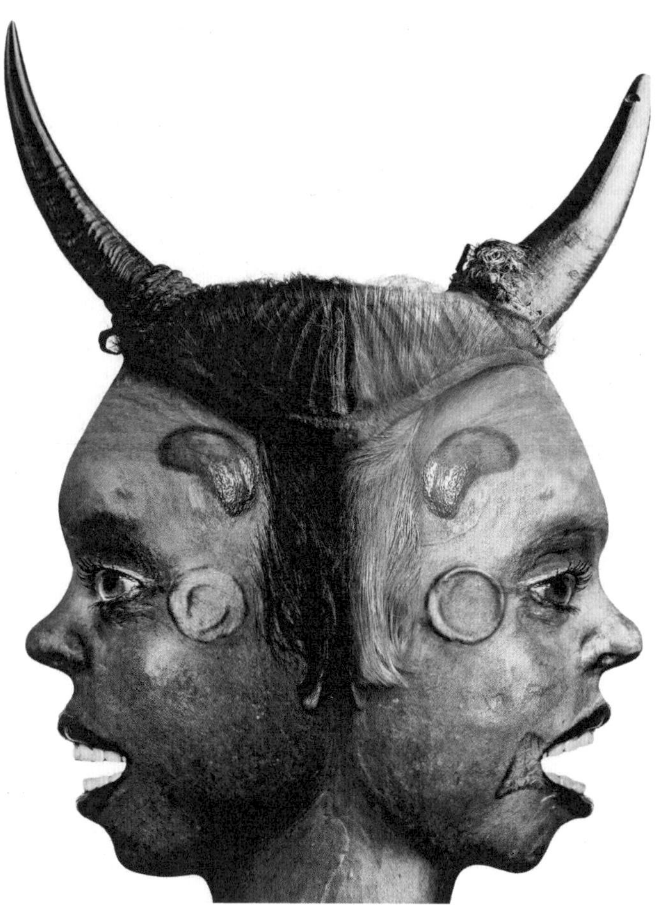

Orlan
Self-hybridation africaine Masque Janus Ekoi Nigeria et visages de femmes Euro-Forezienne, 2003
Digital photography printed on photo paper, 124 x 155.5 cm, ed. 7+1
Courtesy of the artist and Galerie Michel Rein, Paris

constant challenging of the ethical credibility of the figures, their true roles, their emotions and their real dramaturgical function generates generalized uncertainty and doubt about every system of values. This absurd situation makes the perception and evaluation of things impossible and deprives the fundamental orientation of any function because there are no stable, legitimate, permanent links between the different contexts and forms of organization, languages and symbols. With this absurd narrative, a parallel plane is created at the same time upon which the figure of death appears as the victim of a hedonistic world of appearances, as the tragicomic figure of a gigantic simulacrum with no possibility of self-determination, no possibility of playing a true, authentic role. The macabre theatre of the absurd is transformed into a tragic self-revelation of colossal incompetence, of the unstoppable, unavoidable, dramatic loss of any possible orientation, any legitimacy, any simple relationship. The scenery of the unstable, merry, hedonistic, decorative simulacrum of a cynical and risk-free game with death, with the figure of death as an innocuous and grotesque marionette, thus disappears and the real tragedy, the real risk of death and the loss of possibility, of being thrown out into deep, dark and complete irresponsibility, makes its sudden, unexpected appearance.

Gloria Friedmann works here with the tradition of the theatre of the absurd, with elements of the allegories of the dialogue with death or the devil, but above all with the narrative of the revolt against forms of fatalistic determinism that limit if not indeed destroy the possibility of apprehension, the possibility of freedom and self-determination. The alienated bodies and tragicomic marionettes of her simultaneously distressing and ridiculous, macabre, grotesque and deeply disconcerting theatre of exaggerated gestures and absurd relationships create a complex structure of emotionally and intellectually layered references in which the roles constantly change and alter, and the different points of observation draw upon different historical, literary and philosophical discourses. Here a picturesque, fictitious, imaginary space no longer appears as a place, a laboratory for the didactic, experimental demonstration of philosophical, moral and aesthetic reflections, but as the stage of passion and exaggeration, of absurd and impossible dialogues, of simultaneously antagonistic and grotesque juxtapositions, belonging to stylized and archetypal figures. It should be noted how dramatically these pseudo-theatrical spaces work, how dynamic and moving they are in unfolding their own sovereign narrative, both disconcerting and irritating. The dramaturgically modeled and teleologically conceived theatricality of the simulacrum is transformed suddenly, unexpectedly and dramatically into the revelation of the true and distressing tragedy of the loss of responsibility and the impossibility of perception. Our mixed and confused emotions, midway between disgust and anguish, admiration and insecurity, heroism and escape, hope and desperation, heighten our sensitivity to perceive the *nowness of life* and to understand the condition of responsibility as the centre of our orientation.

Hyper-sensorial, mysterious, slightly macabre and psychedelic, the plastic art of Paolo Grassino is informed by analogous radicality of disturbing, dramatic and picturesque theatricality. More than subversive irony, the intellectual and skeptical challenging of conventional roles in a fictitious dialogue between life and death, good and evil, transparency and darkness, we are confronted here with the seductive and stupefying theatricality of anguish, the overwhelming and unbearable premonition of death, the terrifying pathological representation of the cruel transformation of the human into something unknown, incomprehensible and vegetative, where human empathy, responsibility, reason and will no longer exist; where it is fatalistic, indifferent, obscure anonymity, the physicality of the non-human and absolute non-intelligibility that reign.

And yet, in this confusion and agitation, this desperation and disorientation, "there is always, before death, one last chance, which the hero seizes, not death. The hero is he who always glimpses one last chance, who persists in finding possibilities."[6] This exhibition is a tribute to the hero, to the artist, who always finds this last chance.

(2010)

1. Emmanuel Levinas: *Le temps et l'autre*, Presses Universitaires de France – PUF: "*C'est pourquoi la mort n'est jamais un présent. C'est un truisme. L'adage antique destiné à dissiper la crainte de la mort : Si tu es, elle n'est pas ; si elle est, tu n'es pas, - méconnaît sans doute tout le paradoxe de la mort, puisqu'il efface notre relation avec la mort qui est une relation unique avec l'avenir. Mais du moins cet adage insiste-t-il sur cet éternel avenir de la mort.* [...] *la mort est insaisissable,* [...] *elle marque la fin de la virilité et de l'héroïsme du sujet. Le maintenant, c'est le fait que je suis maître, maître du passible, maître de saisir le possible. La mort n'est jamais maintenant. Quand la mort est là, je ne suis plus là, non point parce que je suis néant, mais parce que je ne suis pas à même de saisir. Ma maîtrise, ma virilité, mon héroïsme de sujet ne peut être virilité ni héroïsme par rapport à la mort. Il y a dans la souffrance au sein de laquelle nous avons saisi ce voisinage de la mort - et encore sur le plan du phénomène – ce retournement de l'activité du sujet en passivité.*"

2. Ibid.: "*Ce qui est important à l'approche de la mort, c'est qu'à un certain moment nous ne pouvons plus pouvoir ; c'est en cela justement que le sujet perd se maîtrise même de sujet.*"

3. Emmanuel Levinas: *Entre nous Thinking-of-the-Other*, Continuum, London-New York 2006, p. 92.

4. Emmanuel Levinas: *Le temps et l'autre*, op. cit.: "*Mourir, c'est revenir à cet état d'irresponsabilité, c'est être la secousse enfantine du sanglot.*"

5. Ibid.

6. Ibid.: "*Il y a, avant la mort, toujours une dernière chance, que le héros saisit, et non pas la mort. Le héros est celui qui aperçoit toujours une dernière chance ; c'est l'homme qui s'obstine à trouver des chances.*"

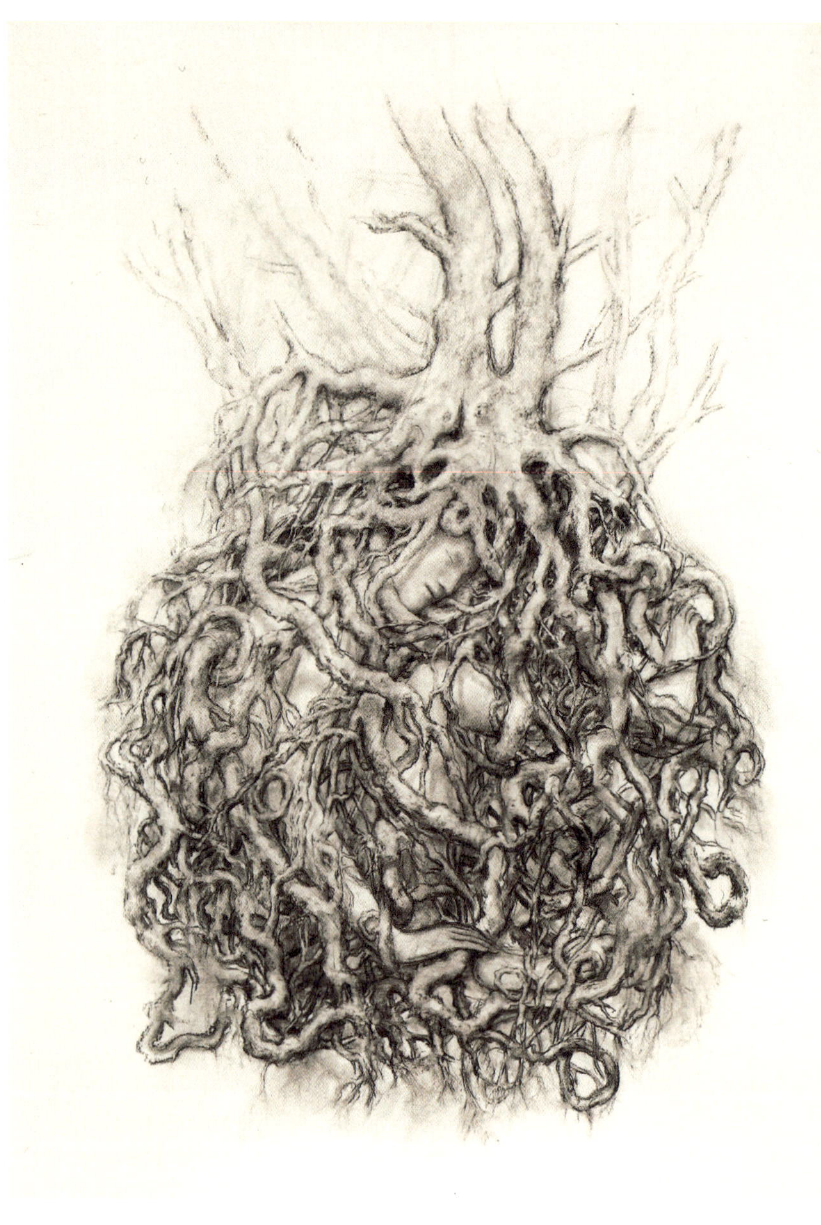

Juul Kraijer
Untitled, 2006-2007
Charcoal on paper, 180 x 125 cm
Courtesy of the artist

INTRIGUING UNCERTAINTIES

Disturbing Narratives

"No person seems better to have understood the secret
of heightening, or setting terrible things, if I may use the expression,
in their strongest light by the force of a judicious obscurity,
than Milton. His description of Death in the second book is admirably
studied; it is astonishing with what a gloomy pomp, with what
a significant and expressive uncertainty of strokes and colouring
he has finished the portrait of the king of terrors. [...] In this
description all is dark, uncertain, confused, terrible, and sublime to the
last degree."
(Edmund Burke, *A Philosophical Enquiry*, 1757)

A certain kind of irresistible, vivid, emotional and adventurous participation in the experience of disturbing improbabilities and uncertainties, in the perception of obscure, irrational, strange and inexplicable phenomena seems to dominate our attitude towards new poetic narratives in contemporary drawing. Sharing in something unexpected, enigmatic and undetermined by conventional logic gives us the intense sensation of discovering – together with the artist, under his guidance – the hidden territory of the abnormal, unusual, exceptional and paralogical. The artist takes on the role of a cicerone who reveals to us the strange and disturbing realities of a *terra incognita* that lives within us, the existence of which is more than clear and evident in all of our attitudes and feelings, in our entire behavior, but at the same time stays hidden, secret and inexplicable by conventional categories and logical systems.

At the same time, we must recognize that these intriguing uncertainties, these disturbing and destabilizing improbabilities, just like the predominance of surprising, excessive obscurities, are not produced merely by the artist's extremely intense and possessive imagination. They are not only creatures of radical and freed fantasy; they are not purely phantasms of the esthetic realm, but very much part of our everyday lives. These uncertainties exist in our daily experiences, in the dreams of our days and our nights. They are present everywhere, demanding attention and recognition; they are clamoring for answers, reactions and dialogue. In this sense, we are their prisoners; we are captives of these "strong subterranean urges," as Dennis Oppenheim once put it in one of his interviews: "it is a fantasy, that art is materialized by a combination of strong subterranean urges and a mysterious field of seduction that connects with primal forces, creating the urge to concretize and communicate. This is all an hysterical fantasy."[1] A connection with "primal forces" involves a deep and dramatic recognition of the capacity and the competence of art to embody experiences that are basic and decisive, though neither visible nor present everywhere. It involves recognition of the disturbing, shocking complexity of the realm of improbabilities and uncertainties, reflecting hidden, undesired realities and referring to unexpected, unforeseen happenings. Dennis Oppenheim was convinced that art conveys a deeper knowledge of these hidden realities through the embodiment of those "strong subterranean urges" that dictate and determine our behavior.

This realm of darkness, chaos, extremes and improbabilities, full of evocations and connotations, of imagination and fears, of vital uncertainties and obscure happenings, is part of our human complexity and of our anthropological reality, as well as of our daily activities and experiences. However, it doesn't reveal itself dramatically and shockingly in every moment or in each situation. Instead, it must be uncovered; it must be liberated through the artist's freed, radical imagination, through extreme, unexpected and disturbing experiences – unforeseen, intense and unusual – that involve a perspective on these hidden realities. The power of evocation, that feeling of the decisive presence of invisible, hidden energies and "strong subterranean urges; " a dramatic recognition of obscure, destructive, frightening forces present in our field of action and even in our emotional universe – it provokes shock, and self-questioning confrontation with undesired realities; it challenges our basic orientation and positioning. This is a cathartic moment and, at the same time, a moment where we recognize our fragility and vulnerability, our inevitable involvement in every context and in every constellation of human, sociocultural complexity. In other words, this is the moment where we recognize our responsibility and engagement, our involvement and participation in the illimitable complexity of all that is happening and all we are doing, in elaborating, changing, shaping and systematizing our reality.

This is the essential duty of the artist: to reveal hidden realities, and to intensify this freed imagination in order to capture "subterranean energies;" to enable the subtle, precise perception of obscurities and improbabilities, and to radicalize the extreme experiences that evoke intriguing, unfamiliar uncertainties; to point to the invisible forces of irrational, unforeseeable, spontaneous occurrences that are present in the context of our everyday *Handlungen* – to use Georg Simmel's word, which refers to the pragmatic and socialized handling and treatment of, and dealing with, the practical and immediate realities of our everyday life and labor.[2] Precisely through this radical, unexpected, unfamiliar and somewhat disturbing, surprising connection between different realms of experiences and different fields of sensibilities, diverse linguistic structures and systematizations manifest themselves as a kind of new consciousness of the complexity of realities, which is capable of recognizing "subterranean urges" and decisive obscurities, and their potential dangers as well as their possibly liberating energies.

Connecting diverse fields of human experience and different systems for their perception creates new perspectives for reading reality; it creates unprecedented and unexpected models for potential combinations of different ways of thinking and diverse ways of transforming the given realities. Through the labor of the artist's intervention, the obscurities, improbabilities and uncertainties become part of our sensibility and imagination. They assume their proper place in our system of orientation, as messengers of another – invisible, unexpected, unknown – *terra incognita*, of an obscure realm of uncertainties, of what we know about and have heard of, but unconsciously don't want to be confronted with. In the materialization of narratives of obscurity, uncertainty and improbability, our real, effective mental and emotional state actually reveals itself through the disturbing, irritating and shocking power of evocative images that allude to the realm of "subterranean urges."

Hannah Arendt's observation that "the last individual left in a mass society seems to be the artist"[3] is more topical than ever, in the sense that these days, only artists seem to be willing and able to embody and convey disturbing, confusing, irritating – and often also undesirable, buried, hidden – improbabilities, obscurities and uncertainties in their work. This is particularly true in our chaotic, confusing times of economic, political and ideological crisis, of dreary and depressing lack of orientation, of fear and insecurity, of ever greater violence and frighteningly commonplace aggression, which paradoxically unfolded immediately following the great illusions of brief and excessive economic prosperity in the middle of the 21st century's first decade. That short-lived and shortsighted, downright blind and definitely arrogant euphoria of consumption on the art market, with its false, unreal, infinitely exaggerated prices and disrespectful investments, speculations and manipulations, suddenly seemed absurd and irrelevant, but above all ethically illegitimate in the moment of crisis. The eruption of a new wave of global terrorism, and the spread and entrenchment of related religious fundamentalism – unwittingly abetted by the mass media and repulsive voyeurism – embodied this profound crisis in horribly brutal images of atrocities and violent excesses that painted an apocalyptic vision of the new century.

In times of crisis and disorientation, more than ever, artists seek to create authentic and poetically effective metaphors in their work, which embody disturbing, confusing, frightening and hidden realities and obscurities, hinting at latent, unforeseen "subterranean urges" and thus visualizing relevant narratives. They concretize, update and reinterpret apparent improbabilities and uncertainties in diverse cultural, mental, linguistic and mytho-

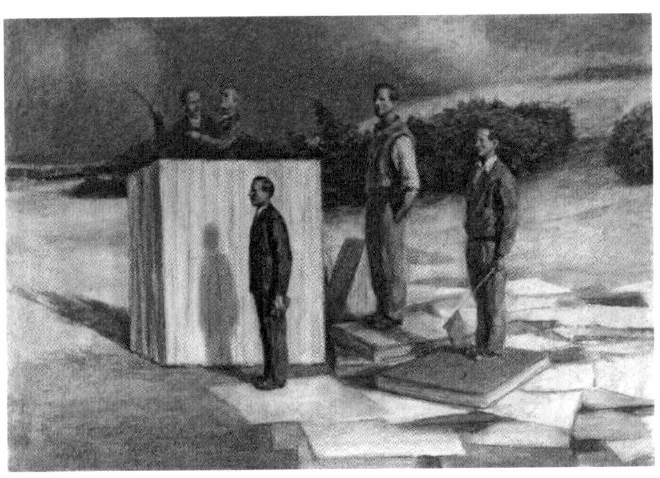

Peter Martensen
Front, 2015
Charcoal on paper, 44 × 64 cm
Courtesy of the artist and Galerie Maria Lund, Paris

logical contexts in such a way that the hidden, potential connections between diverse experiences and systems of representation bring to life new, current and authentic narratives. Sensual, suggestive embodiments of peculiar references to realms and experiences that fundamentally determine our existence – although they cannot necessarily be grasped and understood everywhere, in every situation and in every human constellation – seem to be at the center of the work of the artists taking part in the exhibition "Intriguing Uncertainties – Disturbing Narratives." In this sense, their artistic statements appear to manifest aspects of potential intellectual resistance to the false illusions of the omnipotent, manipulated simulacrum of mass consumer society. With neither critical political statements nor proposals for realpolitik, these artists convey existential, ethical thoughts on our worldview in the form of a permanent exploration of the capacity of art to create authentic, relevant, poetically effective metaphors for uncertainties.

When Hannah Arendt speaks of the artist as the "last individual," she understands "artist" or artistic potential to mean the creative competence, critical independence, individual responsibility and subversive, questioning, freed imagination of the artist, which extends intensively and radically to hidden human realities, fundamental anthropological experiences, and the concealed, impenetrable realms of the experience of obscurities and uncertainties.

In this context, the works of the artists invited to join the exhibition "Intriguing Uncertainties – Disturbing Narratives" appear as particularly authentic and remarkable, since they very radically focus on freeing the imagination, and on contextualizing the visual narratives of improbabilities and obscurities in rich, far-reaching referentiality. The excessive, provocative intensity of the sensual, physical entity of visual creation functions as a subversive, liberating, anarchical and creative force that destroys the ostensible, seductive attractions of the empty, meaningless, superficial and manipulated simulacrum of the world. It deprives this banal spectacle of credibility, and intensifies the vivid cultural, historical, mythological and anthropological connections of artistic narratives. This complex, dense cultural contextualization of the figures of freed imagination visualizes the latent connections between specific, current personal experiences and collective narratives in mythology and the history of mentalities, which convey certain archetypal models of attitudes, hierarchies and value systems.

Many of these artists refer – directly or indirectly – to preformed mythical, historical and conventional imagery, to archetypal stories, cultic and symbolic tales, to metaphorical narratives or to certain magical, paralogical references; to the enigmatic, ritual practices of different cultures and popular traditions; to irrational, unconscious imaginings; to powerful, often alarming, terrifying, wild and merciless images of essential, fundamental and primal experiences that determine the basic orientation of life and manifest directly, without embellishment or sublimation, in archaic, popular and traditional societies. Although this basic orientation is fundamentally significant and directional in communal life, just as it is for our personal behaviors and attitudes, it nevertheless evokes something unknown, unknowable, intangible, insecure and uncertain, something latent and fundamentally true that is actually omnipresent and seems to determine

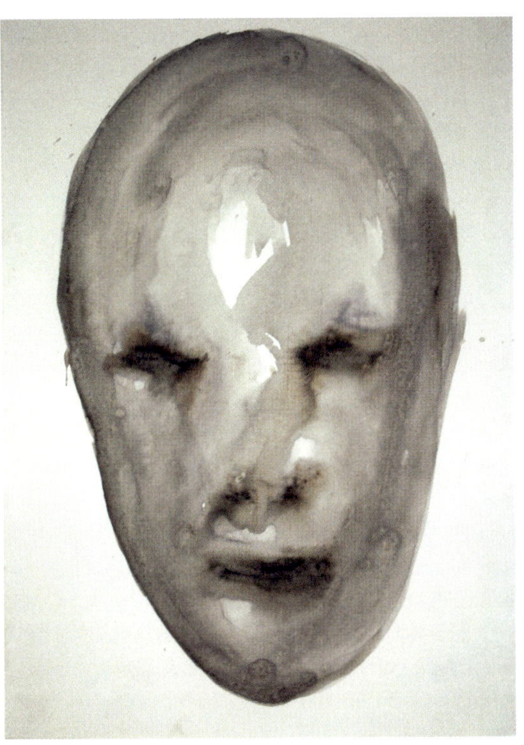

Ugo Giletta
Volto, 2008
Watercolor on canvas, 80 x 60 cm
Courtesy of the artist

infinitely diverse events, even though it cannot be immediately grasped and understood.

Perhaps it is precisely this unbearable, frightening, deeply disconcerting and unsettling uncertainty that brings forth images of an obscure world of inexplicable, opaque and unknowable happenings that suggest a fatal or tragic agnosticism. In these imaginings, something uncertain, enigmatic, inexplicable and improbable is given a tangible body, a discernible image, a sensual appearance that can be experienced and brings to light the profound, invisible and obscure levels of existence. In this sense, these imaginings are utterly radical and almost unbearably severe, effective, embittered, uncompromising and sometimes even merciless, as they refer directly to those elemental experiences that form the basic content of collective narratives and rituals, of popular magic, archaic cultic attitudes and customs.

In the diverse works of art, such fundamentally archetypal, essential and magical narratives – psychological, pathological and paraphysical – are concretized in the context of real, current, personal and immediate experiences, in anthropological constellations, or personified in the context of certain profound, basic value systems and representation models of culture, ideology and mythology present in the contemporary realities of life. Among these are, of course, different concepts of life and death, and of life after death, of body and soul, good and evil, fate and chance, and of the forces and energies, determinations and constellations that shape each individual life. In particular, our feelings about death, and different ideas of the forces related to death that seem to decide on the end of life, generate magical, mythical narratives that have an effect – though often latent and distorted – on our fundamental, profound belief systems.

Cultural, symbolic forms seem just as decisive in the visualization of certain fundamental narratives that determine the metaphorical significance of the great cultural myths, from the story of the golem to Faust and the figure of Frankenstein. The artist's studio, as the place of the enigmatic, mysterious creation of another, alternative and concentrated life, as the special locus of the emergence of an artificial, ergo artistic, specifically intended, fundamentally virtual and imaginary reality – or as Frankenstein's laboratory, the mysterious place of the creation of an artificial creature that can turn against its creator – takes on a metaphorical meaning that allows positive, creative, but also negative, devastating and destructive energies to be virtually freed, and to unfold in the imaginary, fictional reality of a work of art. In the works of several artists in this exhibition, these mythical – or rather, in our times, cultic – places are turned into sites for elaborating authentic metaphors for uncertainties and improbabilities.

The exhibition "Intriguing Uncertainties – Disturbing Narratives" offers diverse personal visions of that tremendous, enigmatic and obscure realm, which is far and near, known and unknown, familiar and unfamiliar at the same time, but which is always with us, because it is within us. There are strange, extremely vivid, almost aggressive moments that burn, torture and profoundly destabilize us in everyone's life and memory, in the present and in the past, in our immediate physical surroundings and in the distant, imaginary territories of our souls. They are resistant to time; they never quit us, and they leave their mark deep in the never-ending chain of events, of our experiences, desires and dreams, in our fear for the future and our horror of the past. These moments, these memories, these obsessions and projections can be so intense and so concrete – psychologically, sensually and emotionally – that it seems that the line between them and so-called real life, or immediate presence, can no longer be clearly identified.

These moments may be our phantoms, our demons; they can occupy our feelings, they can conquer our attention and appeal to our interest to deal with them as we do with any other realities in our immediate, concrete, everyday lives, as we do with any other subjects that seem to be more obviously significant for a given situation in our contemporary lives. Yet they are eminently present in the mental, emotional self of each and every one of us; they are as much forceful and inevitable realities as any other physical or mental element of contemporary life, as any other immediate experience. They are the imaginings of our "self-darkness," as Dennis Oppenheim put it so brilliantly in one of his writings. "An artist's life can be extremely contemplative, introspective. This condition seems to create a secret alliance that makes dark content more accessible, more intriguing. I would be suspicious talking to an happy artist. I'm not sure I'd be terribly interested in what they had to say. Depression is something that seems to figure often in art making, although I don't know that good art is made during anything like clinical depression. It's almost a shamanistic immersion into self-darkness which gives me something usable, something I can reference," he maintained.[4]

When Dennis Oppenheim spoke about "almost a shamanistic immersion into self-darkness," he was referring to an absolutely central element of his artistic thinking, or to put it more accurately, his fundamental approximation of anthropological reality.

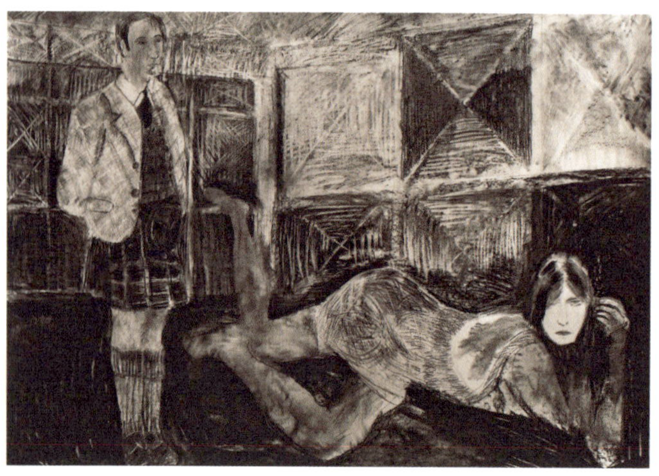

László László Révész
They'll be never connected, 2015
Charcoal and pencil on paper, 152 × 190 cm
Courtesy of the artist

He spoke clearly and positively, and indeed pragmatically and creatively, when he claimed that this fundamentally psychological inclination towards "self-darkness" – which was undoubtedly well thought-out and intellectually contextualized in creative practice – gave him something "usable," creative and practicable. This means that he did not work in a mental state of self-destructive depression. In total consciousness and in full control of his intelligible capacities, his intellectual and esthetic competencies, he instead sought out the creative, liberating, intuitive connections between controlled and uncontrolled, known and unknown, conventional and unconventional areas of experience.

The reference to "almost a shamanistic immersion into self-darkness" describes the artistic competence and capacity to liberate the psychological, intellectual and emotional energy residing deep in the human psyche, and thereby to form new connections between usually disparate realms, forms of energy, spheres and symbolic systems. Dennis Oppenheim deliberately used the "shamanistic" metaphor, without condoning a totally irrational method or approach. He was in no way an irrational artist. On the contrary, he sought to reach for and grasp seemingly inaccessible moments. He worked in consciousness of irrational experiences; he recognized the factual "dark side" as an existing phenomenon, but not as an irrational explanation of all events; not as a generally applicable, negative, unpredictable energy present in deeds and actions, but as part of the human complexity of existence. He wanted to make that "dark content more accessible, more intriguing;" in other words, his was a conscious, clear, liberating stance, a subversive attitude that enabled him to grasp, to ascertain and to know more.

The exhibition "Intriguing Uncertainties – Disturbing Narratives" concentrates on this aspect of contemporary art, on making "dark content more accessible, more intriguing," because our present life, our contemporary society, our real daily experiences force us to confront this realm of human complexity. "The images raised by poetry are always of this obscure kind," wrote Edmund Burke in his famous essay about the sublime. It continues: "In nature dark, confused, uncertain images have a greater power on the fancy to form the grander passions..."[5] Edmund Burke described – in the spirit of the Romantics – the irresistible poetic power of uncertainty, improbability and obscurity, especially because of their capacity to liberate our fantasy, to free our imagination and to create surprising, provocative and shocking connections between spheres and experiences not connected in daily life, in our pragmatic everyday activities. In this sense, Dennis Oppenheim spoke about the subversive and liberating – let's call it creative – role of uncertainty and obscurity: making "dark content more accessible, more intriguing."

The "shamanistic immersion into self-darkness" can be embodied in highly provocative, shocking, disturbing and excessive images that question traditional values, religious dogmas, political symbols or moral conventions, through the deconstruction of language and through the creation of new combinations of allegorical images previously never related, as is done in an extremely dramatic and histrionic way in drawings by Günter Brus. A deeply touching and psychologically complex, painful and dramatic self-interrogation – through ironic and analytical distance from the self as such – forms the narrative of Jim Dine's double portraits with a monkey and a cat, or the triple portrait with the figure of

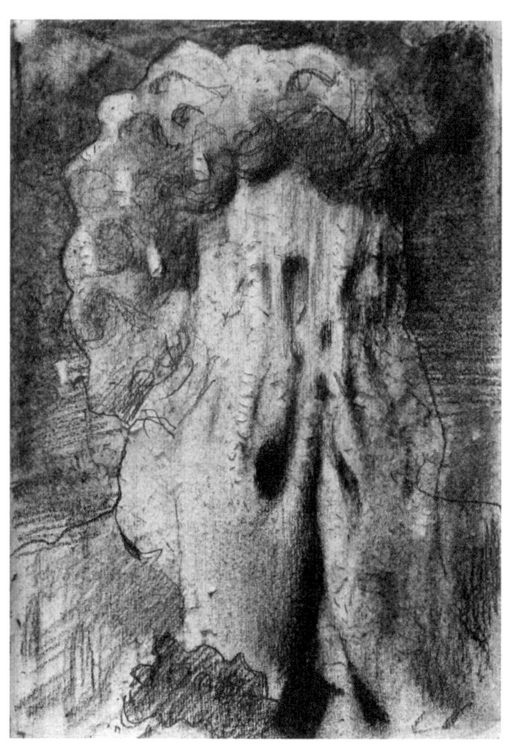

Adrian Ghenie
Pie Fight Study - Drawing 1, 2012
Pencil on paper, 31 × 21 cm
Courtesy Pace Gallery, The Sander Collection, Darmstadt

Pinocchio, in which the subtle, ambivalent, unclear and hardly explicable, rather obscure relationship between the figures emphasizes the eternal instability of human constellations. The evocation of a possible collapse, a likely near tragedy, a probable decline of the fragile, provisional emotional settlement between the unequal actors makes these images sad and dark.

The embodiment of "self-darkness" can be concretized in the dark, empty, abandoned spaces of the artist's studio, where a strange object suddenly appears like an unknown creature sent by somebody else, without any explanation of its origin or the legitimacy of its being in this place at this moment, like Jana Gunstheimer's somber drawings suggest to us. These intriguing stranger-objects question our conventional relationship to works of art, as well as our cultural belief in the role of the artist as master of the creative process. The sudden doubt about the creatures' belonging to the creator; the frightening acknowledgement that something else, something alien, an unknown "stranger" has taken the place of the proper thing that should be here, that should take its rightful place under the competence of the creator – this creates fear, instability, chaos, obscurity and disorientation: all parts of "self-darkness." The enigmatic and irritating transformation of the inner space of the artist's studio or apartment – when suddenly, unexpectedly and inexplicably, familiar objects, working materials or even works created by the artist transform into aliens, into uninvited guests or strangers, and the whole place changes its character and becomes something else, something frightening that points to a realm of "self-darkness" – appears in drawings by Matt Bollinger. His basically clear, well organized and structured spaces suddenly lose their transparent entity; they become obscure and irrational spaces where we lose ourselves, where we lose our orientation and capacity to systematize the chaotic surroundings. Matt Bollinger's drawings, like the works by Jana Gunstheimer, offer an almost classic, rational, transparent order on the surface, but at the same time, they evoke the decisive presence of obscure "subterranean urges," which steer things and events in an unforeseeable, unknown, irritating and destabilizing direction. The clear, transparent surface hints at dark, dangerous and somber perspectives on our human complexity.

The mystery of the – seemingly – empty spaces, and the theater-like arrangement of things in a closed space; the quasi "neutral," unimportant objects on the stage of nothingness, useless, banal and simple, waiting for an event that will never happen; the *horror vacui* of the definitively abandoned, irreversibly emptied, dark and cold, useless and sad territories – they provoke angst and disorientation, destabilization and the feeling of helpless solitude. The architecturally structured, apparently rationally organized, dark and enigmatic space divided into different inner sectors that appears in a monumental drawing by Gianni Dessì conveys the feeling that something could happen in this mysteriously dark space, that some figures, events, motions and intentions could move things; that they could create a change, a real event, real momentum; that they could organize meaningful occurrences and happenings that give meaning to this dark, closed and alienated phenomenon. But the evocation of this event also lets the feeling emerge that perhaps such real momentum doesn't exist at all, and the state of things is eternal waiting; the state of waiting is the only reality that gives meaning to this space.

Maude Maris's stage-like spaces, filled with small, lifeless, simple objects, suggest a similar feeling of emptiness and provoke us to question the hidden, inner, basic forces behind the timeless and silent arrangement, without any movement, any sign of changes, any trace of any will, desire or intention. Her drawings present a world of ontological objectivity: the radical and frightening absence of any subject, decision, movement, change or resistance creates a different form of emptiness devoid of pathos, which introduces us to the realm of "self-darkness."

While Gianni Dessì and Maude Maris explore an enigmatic, inexplicable reinterpretation of seemingly rational, architectural spaces in their drawings, or the presence of potential events in these abandoned spaces that may represent their actual purpose and true function, Alois Mosbacher, Andrea Fogli and Matias Duville work with the evocative, mysterious and irrational levels of meaning in landscapes. Alois Mosbacher shows peculiar, enigmatic formations of natural and artificial, organic and inorganic elements that completely transform the landscape, the forest, the trees in some sort of inexplicable, disconcerting and confusing magic. Everything seems to remain as it was, but an impression of forlornness, of the irresolvable transformation of things destabilizes us and hinders our orientation. Here – as so often in art and literature – forests, nature, trees and meadows are endowed with an obscure, confusing and dangerous entity that metaphorically evokes the unknowability of things.

Andrea Fogli and Matias Duville also work with the motif of landscape, which appears, on the one hand, as a gigantic, monumental battlefield of mutually conflicting energies moved by enormous forces and, on the other hand, as a mystical, enchanted and dangerous place. Matias Duville's large-format draw-

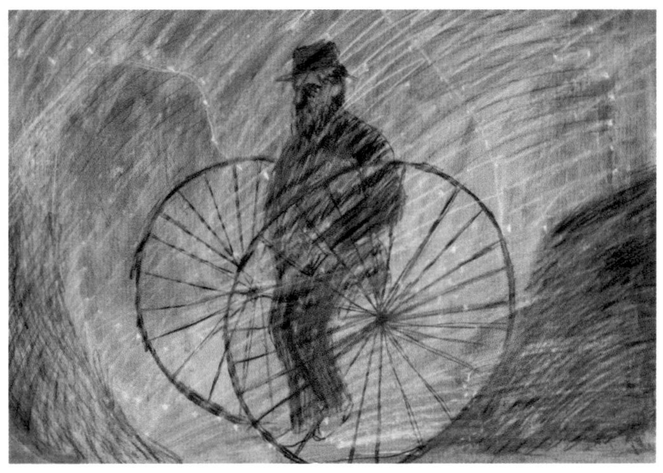

Nicolas Dieterlé
Untitled, 1993-2000
Watercolor and pastel, 39 × 50 cm
Courtesy Galerie Frédéric Moisan, Paris

ings depict wild landscapes where irrational forces wound the earth, tearing open dangerous holes and chasms, or even cutting through mountains and creating formations reminiscent of volcanic eruptions. The landscape transforms into a dangerous and threatening creature, alive with its own will, its own destructive, aggressive intentions and dark impulses.

Andrea Fogli's subtle drawings depict old city parks and manicured gardens where something unnatural and unexpected, something never before seen happens, like a vision that suddenly changes the entire real environment and draws hitherto unremarked, but threatening and frightening apparitions to the foreground. These puzzling transformations completely reinterpret objects and spaces – gardens and fountains, parks and streets – perceived until now as well-known and familiar. Suggesting danger and obscurity, they present the world as a reification of pathological imaginings. A large, dark, threatening vortex, irrationally floating objects or inexplicable sources of light fill the spaces of parks and gardens, rattling our sense of orientation, creating chaos and confusion, and suggesting the fundamental, general and irreversible inscrutability of the world.

Such inscrutability as the world's permanent state is embodied in diverse artistic imaginings, and the ambivalence of all things, the inexplicable transfigurations and irrational events are given a different embodiment of "self-darkness" in each case. Human and animal bodies are merged, creating new, disconcerting, hybrid creatures never seen before. The radical, subversive sensuality of these organic formations suggests struggle and pain, destruction and fragility. The provocative sensuality of the figures of freed imagination, the immediacy of the incontrollable psychological experience; a certain expressiveness and sensuality, a disconcertingly provocative physicality; or the force of the narratives of destruction and violence, of dramatic confrontations, dreary, irredeemable loneliness and marginalization – this unfettered emotionality creates the hyperintense, unsettling aura that fundamentally characterizes Marine Joatton's visual world. The relentless, forceful and dramatic directness of her visual narratives, as well as the physically, sensually tangible materiality of her visual configurations, imbues her drawings with a dramatic force and uncompromising excessiveness that completely immerse the beholder in her visual narratives. Her drastic, profound oeuvre seems to be both archaic and subtly psychological, and its sensual, often brutal, battling and violent figures radiate something peculiar, a somewhat medieval or folkloric, archaic, even slightly primitive aura, while at the same time conveying irrational, complex and psychopathological narratives of the subconscious.

Barbara Eichhorn's dramatic, constantly transforming organic formations in a state of permanent movement resist any definition of affiliation, any attempt to file them in one or the other category of existing beings. At times, these material formations appear as the living bodies of unknown animals, as anatomical structures, or as biological, chemical organisms; at others, they seem to be dynamically moving, self-restructuring matter, forcing itself into different shapes, which appears to know no state of rest, but is in a permanent state of change. Here, forces and energies collide, and matter changes at speed in these monumental drawings that present the world as a place of constant drama and battle, a site of tensions and conflicts.

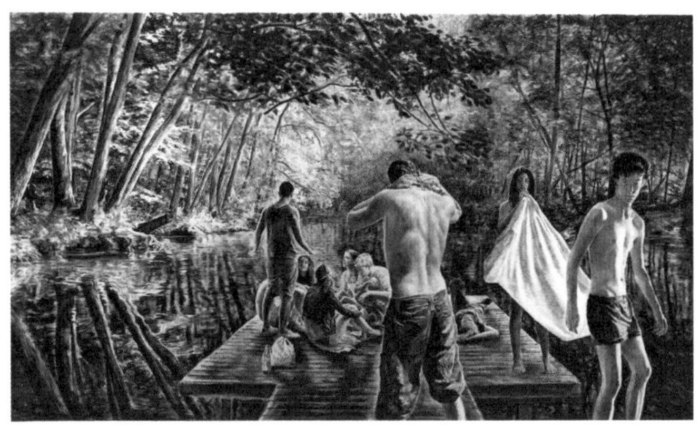

Muntean/Rosenblum
Untitled ("But what did we..."), 2015
White and black pen and acrylic on canvas, 275 × 465 cm
Courtesy of the artists

"Self-darkness" can appear in the unbearable, hysterical irrationality and the chaotic linguistic disorder that unexpectedly drive the inexplicable behavior of people, who seem to be forced to stay on the stage of the theater of improbabilities and obscure dramaturgies, like in the hallucinated movie-like scenes in drawings by Pierre Seinturier, or in the seemingly banal, well-known public places, with their familiar figures and their behavior, that appear in the monumental drawings by Muntean/Rosenblum, who show us a profoundly irritating mixture of well-managed composition and ill-managed literary communication between the actors. In their drawings, Jan Fabre, Pierre Seinturier, Muntean/Rosenblum, Iris Levasseur, Peter Martensen, László László Révész, Andrei Molodkin, Per Dybvig and Nina Kovacheva present obscure scenes of a strange theater of improbabilities and hallucinations, where the dramaturgy of the theater's virtual reality operates with clichés and compositional models of seemingly linear, causal – and literally understandable – happenings, but at the same time reveals the fatal, fundamental and irreversible disorder of all the causalities and all the motivations. The dramaturgically organized events on the stage seem to represent some causal occurrences, motivated by various reasons and intentions. In spite of this apparent normality, the scenes reveal the deep and irreversible absence of any rational explanation for the figures' behavior and actions, the total disconnection between space, time, action and language, and the fatal disorder of the hidden relations between the diverse elements of that crazy scenario. The government of irreversible "self-darkness" dominates this theater of irrationality, dissent and disorder.

The drawings by Kiki Smith, Juul Kraijer, Adrian Ghenie, Oda Jaune, Guglielmo Castelli, Erich Gruber, Ugo Giletta and Lee Bul show diverse visions and artistic, philosophical interpretations of the human body, or of depictions of the body and the face. The common feature of these artistic visualizations of the body and the face lies in the sensibility and orientation of these artists in grasping and showing the buried psychological, mental and intelligible realities of "self-darkness" and "significant uncertainties" hidden behind the façade of everyday, banal and ordinary, pragmatic and logical activities and actions. Juul Kraijer concretizes the frightening, horrifying transfiguration of the human body in the context of certain mythological narratives in her dream-like, hallucinatory, though at the same time enchanting and monumental visions, and considers the body's transformation as a reinterpretation and updating of old horror stories. Meanwhile, Oda Jaune and Erich Gruber work more with psychopathological phenomena, in which the body's destruction or alteration, the creation of new, unnatural bodies or of hybrid formations somewhere between animal and human, or of hybrids of multiple human bodies and members, lead to shocking results of pathological visions. In Oda Jaune's subtle work, we can observe certain reminiscences of Surrealism, but it is above all psychoanalytical experiences that shape her vision of self-awareness and the reification of fear and repression, of dreams and improbabilities, of uncertainty and forlornness.

Ancient ideas of shamanism, the cult of ghosts that appear in the form of animal bodies or in the conglomerations of diverse living beings, appear in Lee Bul's dramatically effective, extremely sensual and powerful depictions of bodies. This vivid, organic, sensual, powerful and enigmatic embodiment of improbability and obscurity emanates mystical, vital energies and blends with other elements and realities. Lee Bul's vision shows a strong connection with communal, popular, cultic and mystical imaginings.

Adrian Ghenie's drawings depict the faces of well-known figures in history and culture, science and philosophy, or his own face, and their psychological, somewhat pathological intensity and deliberate theatricality engage the figures depicted in a different context determined by history, politics, cultural history and the history of mentalities. His figures are not portraits of individual personalities, but instead dramatic visions of historical roles, psychological conflicts, emotional entanglements and sociocultural ambiances that reinterpret the images – the entire mental, psychological and historical complexity of real figures, living or dead, and fictional, imagined figures – as metaphorical embodiments of certain moments, whether historical or purely imaginary.

In their drawings, Oda Jaune, Erich Gruber, Ugo Giletta, Guglielmo Castelli and Adrian Ghenie elaborate sensual embodiments of diverse concepts of the face and the body as metaphors for certain states of existence. While Ugo Giletta seeks total, radical depersonalization and the archetypal essence behind depictions of individual faces, so as to reify the nakedness and vulnerability, fragility and transience of life, Guglielmo Castelli seeks to elaborate vital, relevant situations from the most minute transformations and hybridizations, from the collision and coalescence of small units and microstructures, so as to create possible spaces of survival for his figures. Irrationality, inexplicability and inscrutability dominate their world, where obscurity and "subterranean urges" shape the transformations and reinterpretations of human bodies and faces. Similarly, Ruth Barabash and Felice Levini work with fragments and with lost and found elements that coalesce in fragile, vulnerable, impermanent and enigmatic micro-constellations that cannot easily be penetrated. From this emerge irrational formations that tend to reflect the obscure, unknowable, chaotic aspects of being, rather than suggest any sort of false homogeneity or pseudo-logic, any linearity or explicability of events. "Expressive uncertainty" is embodied in this fragmentary, temporary world of chance and incalculable happenstance.

"Self-darkness" can take the form of violent scenes of black magic rituals and conjurations, or of frightening, obscure voodoo imaginings, in which the personification of Death, cruel fights, the destruction of body and soul determine the entire scenario, like Sandra Vásquez de la Horra, Barthélémy Toguo and Fabien Verschaere tell us in their narratives. In these cruel scenarios of fight and sacrifice, salvation and damnation, the artists often use the imagery of old collective, popular narratives, religious cults, mythological allegories and ethnocultural symbols.

Barthélémy Toguo's anthropological ornamentation, which is suggestive, sensuous and enchanting, colorful and playful, yet simultaneously savage, bewildering and bewildered, frightening, uncontrollable and excessive, visualizes conflicts and struggles, power structures and hierarchies, social roles and working rituals, as well as magical practices, dreams of redemption and liberation, fears of violence and desolation, destruction and demise. In this sense, we may understand his visual-sculptural oeuvre as an extensive, encyclopedic epos unfolding along several parallel pathways, operating with mythical metaphors and rational, socio-critical discourses, and focusing on concrete, collective cultural experiences. What is so impressive and intellectually striking here is that Toguo also operates with a subversive and self-critical, self-reflecting irony that embraces and addresses all the complexity of questions of identity and political engagement in the context of the culture industry. His irony is more a kind of self-irony, with which he challenges the false, defused, kitschy and clichéd images of artists and the art world, or the hypocritical attitudes of cultural consumerism and the neutralizing adoration of the simulacrum.

Barthélémy Toguo has developed a multidisciplinary visual-sculptural language in his art that is complex, powerful and dramatically sensual, and a suggestive, direct, often provocative, violent and potent semiotic system, which also evokes diverse references and various allegorical, symbolic levels of meaning. A constant element in these references is the vital connection to African everyday culture, to present-day African political affairs or African customs, to rituals, acts of magic and sorcery, whereby he always reinterprets and concretizes cultural metaphors in the currently prevailing political, economic and social realms, in dense and diverse situations of cultural, ideological and religious conflict.

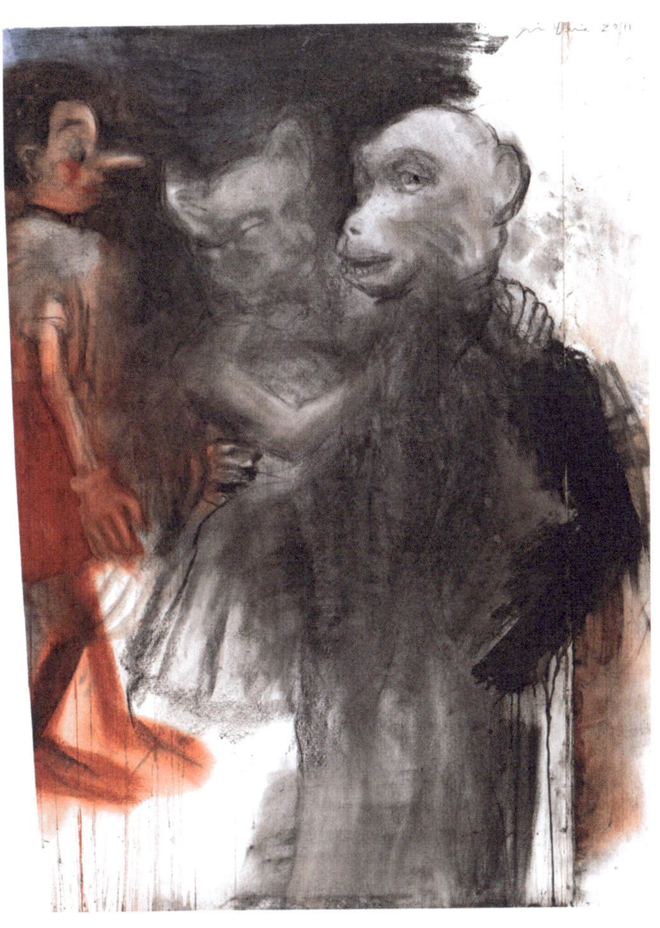

Jim Dine
Walking With Them, 2011
Mixed media on paper, 133 x 101 cm
Courtesy Galerie Templon, Paris and Bruxelles

Alarming and terrifying, barbaric and exotic, insistent and seductively physical, enigmatic, hallucinatory and eerie – such is the effect created by Sandra Vásquez de la Horra's drawings. Her picturesque, subversive fantasies unfold in a dense, obscure world of malevolent, unpredictable, often aggressive and violent beings whose physical identities, morphological affiliation, intentions and motivations remain fundamentally incomprehensible. The beholders are confronted with the constant, unsettling and destabilizing transformation of the figures, and these organic, plant-like, animalistic or human figures resist any attempt at identification. They insist on being perceived in precisely this fluid, mysterious state of irrational, inexplicable transformation situated outside any conventional, understandable logic. Nothing is impossible; it is improbabilities, above all, that are given sensual and organic embodiment, making the poetic competence of magical narratives appear as utterly evident, matter of course, everyday reality. This light, natural, even naïve way of dealing with the realm of magic, with ideas and hallucinations of improbabilities, reinforces the magical, cultic and paralogical quality of the narratives, which integrate irrational coalitions and transformations into events as absolutely matter-of-course elements of everyday experience.

The matter of course presence of irrational, fantastical, magical and surreal elements within a tangible, sensual, material and physical reality – where violence, sexuality, emotionality, irony and malevolence, physical immediacy and radical imagination are seamlessly integrated into anecdotal narratives – places the visual worlds of Sandra Vásquez de la Horra and Barthélémy Toguo in the vicinity of magical, enchanted, surreal stories in African and South American folk culture, folk tales and folk songs, legends and poems, in which the lines between empirical experiences and fantastical, dream-like, irrational improbabilities are completely blurred. These artists often create figures that also exist in the mental and spiritual context of conventional, collective beliefs and imaginings of folk culture – colorful and picturesque, but also obscure, mysterious and irrational – and most particularly those that reify fears or common images of death, illness or malevolent spirits.

Something popular and archaic, something conventional, some part of the collective and communal unconscious also seems to be at work in these artists' drawings. Sandra Vásquez de la Horra, Barthélémy Toguo and Fabien Verschaere tell us not only their individual, personal and particular imaginings and dreams, but work with the dense fabric of folkloric, magical and hidden, collective and religious ideas, and thus in the archetypal, conventional and popular context of ancient metaphorical stories. They radicalize them, insofar as they put greater emphasis on certain contemporary orientations and sensibilities, certain current concretizations, placing these at the center of their narratives. They thus elaborate these archetypal, magical, folkloric and irrational motifs in new contexts that convey the ideas and suspicions, anxieties and fears of our era. By this, they reinforce the psychological orientation of the narratives: sexual, pathological and self-destructive imaginings manifest more openly and directly, and the ironic, even skeptical, critical and subversive questioning of certain ancient, traditional beliefs and magical or religious ideas takes on an important role in the narratives.

These inexplicable, mystical, but also exciting transformations and transgressions that can be experienced with the senses and the imagination, as well as the constant penetration and unstoppable, intriguing and complex coalescence of the elements involved, create an hallucinatory, psychological and sensual intensity of fantastical, often subconscious connotations. They stoke our desire to take part in this dark, magical world that is nowhere near as harmless, free of conflict, gentle and fairytale-like as we might imagine it to be at first glance.

We are dealing here with the extremely exciting, complex and contradictory process of the creation of an authentic narrative, which both operates with the real, genuine material of popular, archaic and metaphorical stories, and subversively questions them, or consistently radicalizes and reinterprets them. On the one hand, the magical, irrational, paralogical and elemental force of the imagery is confirmed – thus leading to a functional redefinition of visual art in the realm of archaic sorcery, popular, folkloric black magic and irrational, paralogical, hallucinatory collective experiences. On the other hand, precisely this magical, imaginary and inexplicable improbability is relativized as theater, as artificiality, as an intentional narrative, poetically fashioned and subversive, emphasizing the allegorical nature of the scene and the plot. This allegorical nature, or the subversive deployment of suggestive, archetypal elements of popular magic, unleashes subversive potential and creates a powerful, poetically effective and psycho-emotionally authentic narrative, in which ancient magical imaginings are transformed into topical, telling and radical metaphors for our contemporary orientations and sensibilities.

Monumental, dark and sensual visions of the eternal black magic wielded by unknown and unpredictable figures that rule the world pour out in an unstoppable tide of images. Their movements and gestures, their manipulations and obscure rituals foster an atmosphere of fear and horror – but nonetheless, a hidden, ironic voice may point out that it is all perhaps just an allegorical performance, a subversive imitation; that maybe, we are merely dealing with some sort of mystical, enchanted theater, even if this play approximates the realities of inexplicable, boundless cruelty, irrationality, self-destructiveness and manic self-destruction in an alarming and terrifying way.

Such chaotic, quasi-ritual presentations of densely agglomerated, irrational events are similarly characteristic of the visual worlds of Fabien Verschaere and Barthélémy Toguo, whose works refer to certain popular, folkloric, medieval or African visual narratives, as they are of Sandra Vásquez de la Horra's drawings. Their drawings convey a colorful, particular and fantastical narrative in which ancient, folkloric tales merge with completely new, contemporary stories shaped by the pathology of contemporary life. It is astonishing how easily and naturally the diverse layers of meaning intermingle. In their drawings, the artists create a provocative, eclectic, quasi-mythological visual world that is contemporary par excellence, and that integrates various subcultural elements, aspects of urban living and spontaneous visual fantasies, just as well as connotations from art history. This picturesque, somewhat confusing visual world – both banal and refined, ironic and poetic – unfolds boundlessly and unstoppably, like a vegetal organism that absorbs and assimilates all elements and things. The various figures and scenes from diverse, imaginary stories of our contemporary simulacrum of a world are thus blended and combined with references drawn from the context of art history, from works of literature and from mythological traditions.

Nearly all the motifs, figures, visual elements and topoi that appear in these artists' drawings and paintings come from different

collective, communal semiotic systems and well-known visual legacies, from conventional visual realms, and from historical and cultural or contemporary, subcultural contexts. The decisive element is the specific reinterpretation of motifs and figures, uprooting them from their history, and their unsettling transfer into other contexts, their combination with foreign elements, and their integration into new iconographic systems.
Remarkably, this eclectic, heterogeneous visual world that is quintessentially contemporary manifests great coherence and poetic effectiveness, as the artists have found a genuine, authentic, honest and self-evident form of a potentially new, narrative and visual language that effectively reflects our eclectic everyday culture. The apparent ease of visual representation, the easily legible, sometimes decorative and ornamental formation of the series of drawings, and the natural, self-evident nature of the eclectic motifs combine to form a visual language that reflects our real, pathological experiences.

While Fabien Verschaere's, Sandra Vásquez de la Horra's and Barthélémy Toguo's visual worlds refer to diverse, communal, folkloric and collective forms of expression, be they medieval, religious or contemporary and subcultural, the subtle, irrational narratives in drawings by Christian Lhopital and Veronika Holcová are shaped by pathological phenomena, and unfold instead in the realm of personal imagination and the psychological inwardness of the lonely individual. Christian Lhopital's graphic works present a dense, vivid and pulsating, constantly reforming and restructuring world of diverse happenings, which is effusive, vibrating, elemental and colorful, unfolds at several levels and in different places, and develops in diverse directions, showing the permanent, inexorable transformation of manifold beings. Mysterious figures and inexplicable, irrational, enigmatic events populate the dynamically fluctuating, dense, virtual spaces of these works. The figures' permanent metamorphosis creates a sort of hyperintense instability and hallucinatory suspension above solid objects and spaces. Everything appears fluid, morbid, gentle and undefined. At the same time, however, strong, monumental and aggressive gestures and movements crystallize, indicating the constant presence of a powerful potential for violence. At any moment, the small, personified beings in hiding, the faces and eyes that seem very concrete, sharp, fast, personal and immediate, the aggressively acting, unpredictable shapes and the malevolent, ghostly figures may break free from any system, from any order, to execute their powerful actions freely, with no control or limitation whatsoever. What we experience here is a permanent psychological state of emergency, in which the rules of predictability have been invalidated, as have all other systems. Christian Lhopital and Veronika Holcová have succeeded in representing the state of insubstantiality, which principally evokes an ethical quandary, as a state of absence of any system, a state of defenselessness and vulnerability. This psychological nakedness, this state of being unprotected and at the mercy of external forces, this extreme vulnerability is given shape not in the obviously brutal, excessive acts of violence of the great heroic narratives, but instead in a hidden, often deliberately concealed lack of orientation, in almost unnoticeable waves of fear, danger and uncertainty, in dark moments of terrible loneliness, futility and desperation within the frameworks and structures hitherto thought to be stable.

Christian Lhopital's serial drawings convey this feeling of permanent, irresolvable, irreversible and inevitable instability, vulnerability and insubstantiality, which can in effect be perceived as the state of things. This insubstantiality and fluidity, and the amorphous, obvious indefinability of the coalescing, living and organic forms, suggest a state of existence marked by permanent, spontaneous, vegetative and unconscious, unreflecting transformations, in which the criteria and definitions of those affected are completely overruled. What the beholders are confronted with is a permanent process of transformation: the biological and vegetative, sensual and material coalescence of the diverse beings and enigmatic figures that populate these fictional, imaginary spaces and obscure, confusing places. Fragments of human bodies, faces, eyes and mouths; animal bodies, plants, flowers and fruit; geographical formations and invented, imaginary, surreal figures – they all coalesce in unusual, unreal and unnatural formations that are nonetheless energetic, pulsating and alive, and the faces, in particular the eyes, engage in immediate, direct, hyperintense and unsettling communication with the beholders.

Sometimes, it seems as if the individual motifs, the strange small figures, the improbable yet energetic, lively beings in this enchanted, effusive, colorful and obscure world of constant tension and excessive intensity are communicating directly with the beholders, and as if they could reveal the mysteries of this magical world. Their ironic gaze meets the eye of the beholder, who constantly seeks to know their nature and their fate, the meaning of their lives, their vocations and their secrets, without ever receiving an unambiguous answer. This deliberate openness to interpretation is nevertheless always combined with psychological, direct and inner experiences; it remains consistently vital and elemental, flavored with a slight, intelligent, subtle and manipulative irony. The artist directs his eccentric puppet theater and allows black magic, sorcery or psychopathological stories to unfold. At the same time, however, he reveals these – through irony and by casting doubt on the credibility of the theatrical dramaturgy – to be artificial, intentional and seductive manipulations of the artifact: fictional, imaginary, metaphorical reality. This poetically articulated and sensual, playful obscurity constitutes, at the same time, the intentional effectiveness of this mimetic theater, and of the genuine, concealed, irrational and uncontrollable psychological processes inside us, our "self-darkness," which forces us to engage in metaphorical sublimations instead of real, immediate and forceful actions. The tension between the real obscurities, the authentic embodiment of "self-darkness," the gigantic dimensions of pathological depth, and the theater's intentional, deliberately playful artificiality endows Christian Lhopital's poetic world with unsettling ambivalence, dramatic force and disconcerting pathos.

Similarly, irony, irrationality, ambiguity and a certain theatrical, pathos-laden, emotional confusion are characteristic of Veronika Holcová's work. Accordingly, the masterfully playful, ostensibly light, decorative and ornamental surfaces of her graphic works exhibit a similar psychological complexity and ambivalent, provocative irony as the works by Christian Lhopital – both artists operate with affecting, unsettling, even frightening intimations of irrational imaginings. Their artistic, playful, or ironically relativized presentation of emotional conflicts and irrational, inexplicable visions drawn from the subconscious creates both a comical – or tragicomic – dramaturgy of the soul, not to be taken seriously, and a deeper level of the interconnected and coalescing emotions and their sublimations that is seriously disconcerting, complex, often pathological and alarming. While Christian Lhopital develops an utterly subtle, fragile, dream-like and exotic visual literature in his folios, Veronika Holcová tends to work with references to art history drawn from late Romanticism, with connotations taken from the literary culture of Symbolism, and with hints at various forms of somewhat decadent Art Nouveau, as well as the soulful Secession, and irrational Metaphysical Art and Surrealism. The presentation of different events reminiscent of theater and of inexplicable happenings creates a rich, far-reaching and uncontrollable aura of association, in which fragments of imaginary stories, scenes of – deliberately stylized – black magic, hints at sorcery and paraphysical manipulations are blended with serious, dramatic and emotional content to create a suggestive, expressive world of illusion.

Veronika Holcová invites the beholders to be touched, first and foremost, by the power of the phenomenon, the weight of the facts, the pure dimensions of intangibility. The emotional effectiveness of this encounter with the indescribable complexity of existing beings and figures becomes even more dramatic as we realize the impossibility of definitions, the lacking capacity and limited nature of our methods of perception. The constant coalescence of figures, the continuous transformation of configurations, and the incessant reinterpretation of their functions and contexts, as well as the impossibility of localizing them, or of defining their origins and their movements, unsettle our orientation within the multitude of realities. Not only do we fail to grasp these exotic, picturesque and indescribable phenomena, we also cannot understand the meaning of their transformations. Here, improbabilities are given bodies, flesh, color, materials, dimensions and power.

In this sense, artistic practice is a reification of our complicated, tortured and contradictory relationship with the "primal forces" that ultimately determine our attitudes, our actions

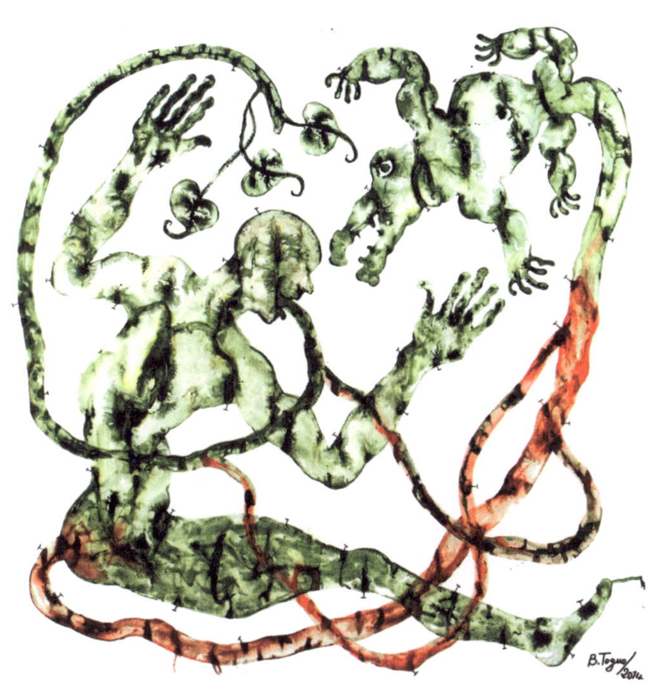

Barthélémy Toguo
Natural Song, 2014
Watercolor mounted on canvas, 240 × 240 cm
Collection du Musée d'art moderne et contemporain de Saint-Etienne Métropole

and our fate. It is a visualization of the "mysterious field" that creates a connection to the "primal forces," and thus the materialization of a narrative that contains our fundamental human orientation. That is why there is actually no point in attempting to analyze the individual pages of this enigmatic encyclopedia. Its actual meaning – its powerful, poetically effective and dramatic message – lies precisely in its exaggerated, almost obsessive, encyclopedic nature, in the irritating incomprehensibility of its variety, and in the great emotionality that accompanies the feeling of the sublime. This holds true especially for the moment in which we perceive its overwhelming dimension of mysteriousness and its ontological fluidity, which resist any attempt at a morphological formalization of this illimitable variety, any simplification of the enigmatic impenetrability – though certainly real, sensual, practical and material – of human constellations and their cultural, symbolic forms, which sublimate the "primal forces" in the cultural, symbolic, collective and conventional context, making them bearable.

Perhaps "strong subterranean urges and a mysterious field of seduction" might explain the mystifying connections between different objects and figures, the mysterious combinations of forms from nature, quasi-architectural fragments, immaterial visions and artifacts, with no rationalistic reasons behind the transfiguration that seems to be a state of being. Influenced by well-known references to art history as well as lesser-known imaginary inventions, the breathtaking, confusing, even baffling variety of transfigurations, and of continuous, disconcerting, psychopathological, cultural and symbolic transformations of organic formations, figures and natural things into other kinds of beings – as well as the related, divergent interpretations – manifest a quasi-ontological fluidity that refers not only to the experience of limitation in morphological descriptions of these transformations. It also points to the untenable, indefensible dependence of our capacity for reception on various typological models for orientation in the world.

Veronika Holcová's enigmatic, exotic, peculiar and confusing encyclopedia of improbabilities – her direct, courageous, provocative and unconventional exploration of the issues of cultural, historical and metaphorical contextualization in such an encyclopedia – presents us not only with unexpected, unforeseen transfigurations and a masterly, profound, almost bleak depiction of the incalculable events of "primal forces." It is also an authentic, legitimate consideration of the potential applicability of morphological typologies, even though the fluidity of the figures and the unpredictability of the configurations seem to negate any possibility of a comprehensible genealogy. It is a triumph of artistically, sensually and imaginatively suggestive improbabilities, since – confusingly – they very much do evoke vital, fundamental, anthropological probabilities hidden deep in our psyche.

Although they operate with very different sociocultural and historical references, the visual narratives by Allison Hawkins,

Nicolas Dieterlé and Didier Trenet similarly convey a feeling of constant fluidity, transience and instability, of the inexorable and inevitable changeability of things, spaces and places. It is a feeling that all and any lines are blurred between dreams and everyday life, present and past, personal experiences and collective, cultural memory. Everything seems suspended in a state of constant – and fundamental, unchangeable, ontological – flux: all the motifs, such as landscapes, animals, architecture and above all human figures, are caught up in eternal and quasi-objective, fundamental transformation, or rather transfiguration. The substantial, semantic and emotional coherence of these visions of restless, boundless and relentless dreaming blends with the normalcy and commonness of the banal events of random, regular everyday life, in which the dreamlike, fantastical, enchanted and irrational entity of the visual phenomena evokes another, mysterious, hidden and intangible level of reality.

While Allison Hawkins weaves her childhood memories of life in America's rural Midwest into her dreamlike presentations, French artists Nicolas Dieterlé and Didier Trenet work with references to cultural history, as well as literary and architectural motifs, which connect their poetic, evocative oeuvre with the spiritual sensibility, empathy and pessimism of Romanticism, or with Mannerism's delight in ambivalence, doubt, agnosticism, and hiding behind a variety of masks. Continuous transfiguration plays a central role in the graphic oeuvre of both Didier Trenet and Elmar Trenkwalder, in particular the transformation of architectural forms into human bodies. Didier Trenet visualizes a worldview consisting in irony and pathos, melancholy and doubt by reinterpreting architectural fragments from manneristic and baroque – heroic – landscape painting, and by both revering and exposing nostalgic heroism. For his part, Elmar Trenkwalder tends to explore the psychoanalytical and pathological tradition of quintessentially Central European culture, seeking to reify relevant metaphors for our contemporary doubts as to the cognoscibility of the fundamental connections between illusion and reality.

Obscurity, unforeseeable destiny, inexplicable decline of goodwill and optimism; predominance of uncertainties, which make our orientation almost impossible and force us to continue to question all the seemingly stable values and conventions, and which reveal dark and dolorous experiences behind mythological narratives, behind religious rites and the diverse forms of strange, irritating magical practice – all these subjects tend to find their authentic, suggestive, powerful metaphoric embodiment, which works through its highly intensified sensual entity. No matter whether it is evidently referential, contextualized in the symbolic forms of cultural communities or traditions, religious or cultic conventions, or extremely unprecedented and completely unforeseeable, the poetic power of the broad, solid and profound foundation of metaphor conveys revelations of decisive force and determining influence to our consciousness. These powerful metaphors reveal the realm of the hidden realities that guide us and shape our possible actions and behavior.

The idea for the exhibition "Intriguing Uncertainties – Disturbing Narratives" was born during the last year of Dennis Oppenheim's life, when we prepared his long-planned one-man-show at Musée d'Art Moderne de Saint-Étienne. During the long years of our beautiful friendship, we met at so many different places where we worked together on various projects, from Sarajevo to Vienna, from Budapest to Rome, from Valencia to Palermo. I invited him several times to make exhibitions at different museums and foundations, or I followed him to cities to see his shows and to meet him in always changing situations, together with different friends, colleagues and other artists. Frequently I accompanied him to places where I really wanted to see his work *in situ*, and to understand his very complex ideas about the immediate and vital relation to the real, concrete human context, but also the solid and unchangeable foundation of his – let's call it – "inner narrative," which was actually his concept of the hidden psychological and emotional mechanisms and motivations of human attitudes.

When I first spoke to him about the one-man-show I had wanted to realize in Saint-Étienne for a long time, he immediately mentioned that as a young man, he had admired old Expressionist films from the 1920s and early 1930s, where a kind of permanent demonization of human nature, or rather the powerful exaggera-

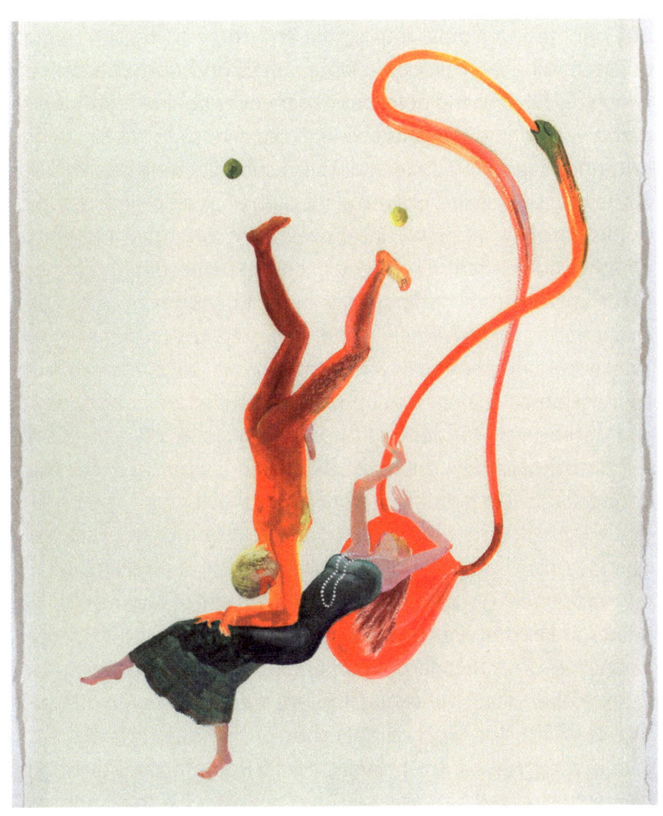

Veronika Holcová
Diary Records, 2008-2011
Oil on handmade paper, 42 × 29 cm
Courtesy of the artist

tion of the uncontrollable, hidden, irresistible drivers of human behavior, was often a central element of the dramaturgical structure. Actually this was the narrative he wanted to emphasize in the planned exhibition in France. We slowly developed the idea of the show in several discussions and exchanges, and we also considered the subject as a possible basis for a great exhibition with a lot of other artists and perhaps even films.

At the time, I was working on another big show for Palazzo Riso in Palermo, where Dennis also participated with a very impressive light installation, which used very intense, playful but also symbolic light effects and operated with mechanical motion, with a kind of industrial production, with the image of a factory, and with the effect of mechanical repetition. The Palermo exhibition in the beautiful, solemn, dark 17th century baroque palace was called "Essential Experiences – Time, Death, Responsibility, Radicalism"[6] and explored the artist's capacity to concentrate on certain fundamental issues that determine our principal orientation and emotional condition in the universe, as Emmanuel Levinas reflected on the subject.[7]

Dennis was deeply interested in my – as he said ironically: Central European, meaning decadent, melancholic and pessimistically realistic – interpretation of his work, which offered an alternative to the eternally repeated pattern of "body art, conceptual art, land art, environmental engagement" that he opposed and vehemently refused. In our discussions, he often also mentioned my European – or Central European – way of thinking, which evidently followed other systems, other codes and references, other models of operating with cultural metaphors and symbolic forms than the American way of systematizing methods, materials, structures and their "technical origins," as Dennis called them. He always welcomed my non-technocratic views on art and my search for deeper levels of narratives. During the finalization of the Palermo show, we had time to discuss the new project I had named "Intriguing Uncertainties – Disturbing Narratives."

I tried to concentrate more and more on the questions of "self-darkness" and the "uncertainties," which most strongly attracted my interest in the essay by Dennis, and at the same time, in the brilliant and astonishing essay by Edmund Burke published in 1757, *A Philosophical Enquiry into the Origin of our Ideas of the Sublime and Beautiful*, in which he speaks about the esthetic power of obscurity and uncertainty.[8] Dennis' expression of "self-darkness" and Burke's repeatedly mentioned categories of "obscurity" and "incomprehensible darkness" both focus on human reality, on the psychological, emotional drivers of human actions and attitudes, on the "despotic governments" of our behavior. They both concretize and localize the effect of "self-darkness" and "judicious obscurity" at the center of the poetic power of works of art. When writing about Milton's representation of

Death, Burke emphasizes the "force of a judicious obscurity": "His description of Death in the second book is admirably studied; it is astonishing with what a gloomy pomp, with what a significant and expressive uncertainty of strokes and colorings he has finished the portrait of the king of terrors."[9] In Burke's conception, obscurity, uncertainty and confusion are evidently connected with the sublime, and create stronger effects than clearness, rationality and knowledge: "Sublimity is principally due to the terrible uncertainty of the things described... The images raised by poetry are always of this obscure kind."[10]

In any case, my original idea was to make a strange, poetic, somewhat mysterious and enigmatic, obscure and passionate exhibition of drawings with strong, disturbing and interrogating narratives; only drawings that manifest a certain kind of intimate, hidden, personal "writing" character, even if they are sometimes relatively precise preparatory drawings, quasi "plans" for future works or future urban, architectural spaces and settlements; dark imaginings of potential special arrangements that involve dreams, fears and dangers, as well as positive utopias about possible future architectural organizations. Of course, Piranesi inspired me at least as much as the early modernist, utopian architectural drawings by Antonio Sant'Elia, Hans Poelzig, Bruno Taut and Hans Scharoun, as well as the glass architecture or Alpine architecture of the euphoric group of young avant-garde German architects of the "Glass Chain," with their utopian space poetry and transparent, hanging dream-buildings.

Evidently, I got further strong inspiration for exploring the "subterranean energies," the "subterranean urges," the "despotic governments" and the irrational, subconscious, incontrollable, unexpected drivers of human relations, attitudes and behaviors behind seemingly rational attitudes and models, and behind conventional, mechanical structures of communication and value representation, from Picabia's, Duchamp's and Man Ray's works from the early 1920s, from drawings, paintings, objects and mechanical instruments that objectified human attitudes and their latent, hidden guidance. From this perspective, Man Ray's object "L'homme" from 1918 and the preparatory drawing for the piece from 1917 appear especially significant, because they manifest one of the basic esthetic ambitions of the entire war generation of intellectuals, artists, writers, photographers and movie-makers: to find an adequate metaphor for the mechanical, machine-like "new human," who was actually the product of the first "modern" war. The seemingly transparent, rational, mechanical system of machines indirectly reveals the basically and principally irrational, obscure motivations of decisions and attitudes, namely the destructive, dark energies of modern society and its modern humans.

These are the "self-darkness" and the "subterranean urges" Dennis Oppenheim focused on in today's modern America; this is the "judicious obscurity" and the "significant and expressive uncertainty" Edmund Burke described in Romantic England; this is the seemingly rational systematization of the – public, common, conventionally organized – sociocultural space that Dada subversively de-constructed and delegitimized. The artists working in this field of making "dark content more accessible, more intriguing" are aware of the risks of history, chaos, disorder and collapse. They are dancing at the edge of the stage. Jan Fabre's drawings, installations, dance performances and plays demonstrate this extremely risky artistic enterprise between madness and clarity, between hysterical hallucinations and deep visions of "self-darkness," which demands complete participation and offering up of oneself. Günter Brus's provocative, excessively violent visual-textual hybrids; Hermann Nitsch's drawings of mysterious rituals, of salvation processes and anatomical inquiries into the interior of the body as metaphors of Orpheus's journey in the Labyrinth; Erik Dietman's suggestive, evocative, shocking bodies blending humans and unknown, frightening species; Marine Joatton's unidentifiable beings, with their aggressive, vivid, offensive demands for their proper space – without declaring their intentions and their tendencies, they all speak of the "subterranean urges" and "despotic governments" that seem to determine our attitudes and gestures. When Hermann Nitsch operates in the extremely complex cultural context that includes the Greek tradition of tragedy as well as its congenial interpretation by Friedrich Nietzsche, the medieval Christian popular trials and mystery theaters, he is using existing cultural metaphors and symbolic systems in a subversive, liberating way, in order to free all radical imagination to create new, unconventional, surprising and authentic connections between the past and the present, between diverse collective, ritual conventions and contemporary psychological interpretations, between varied cultural codes and symbolic forms. In this new, contemporary form of a "total work of art," Hermann Nitsch speaks to the very contemporary emotions and considerations of "self-darkness" and "subterranean urges."

This very conscious focus on "self-darkness," this capacity to catch any moment of "self-darkness" and "expressive obscurity," this ability to reveal the anthropological reality behind any illusion of harmony and rationality changes the sensibility of the recipient and breaks the illusions of rationalism. Through irony and absurdity, transparency turns obscure, the rational turns irrational, and harmony turns into chaos. That's why Dennis Oppenheim rejected all kinds of formal "cleanness" and simplicity, which fail to do justice to real human complexity, ambiguity and contradictoriness; that's why Edmund Burke said, "In reality, a great clearness helps but little towards affecting the passions, as it is in some sort an enemy to all enthusiasm whatsoever."[11]

The exhibition "Intriguing Uncertainties – Disturbing Narratives" continues the artistic exploration of authentic narratives, and of the competence and capacities of art, in elaborating appropriately subtle, empathetic systems "to create a secret alliance that makes dark content more accessible, more intriguing," as Dennis Oppenheim put it. There is also a certain personal aspect to this exploration: my father was an architect. In my early youth, I also wanted to be an architect, and I still keep in my mind a vision of his office with architectural drawings everywhere in structured disorder, where only he knew the cartography of the various plans, some of them in the form of expressive "sketches," as he called his small drawings of the first ideas for future buildings. Already at that time, I was thinking about this strange, strong ambiguity and contradictoriness: order and disorder, architectural rationalism and creative chaos; clear, concrete, specific ideas of space and a somewhat obscure, uncertain, evocative and imaginative aura that lent a vivid, human, almost sensual reality and dynamic vitality to the rationally organized and objectively executed architectural plans and drawings.

Strangely, I rediscovered this exciting, complex feeling when I visited Dennis Oppenheim's studio for the first time. After so many years of professional life and work as an art historian in many different cities and a number of different countries, I suddenly found myself deep in my past, in the confusing and emotionally moving memory of my father's half-dark studio, with the old volumes of *Handbuch der Baukunst* and *Architekturgeschichte der Welt* inherited from my grandfather, who was actually also an architect and an architecture historian. His illustrated books filled the high bookshelves in my father's studio, where I spent long hours and days admiring this treasure trove of ideas, images, forms and stories, where I imagined the old cities with their palaces and towers, castles and bridges, streets and squares, with their people and their feelings, attitudes and behavior.

I still love architecture very much, and I think I understand very well Dennis' intention to reveal the emotional, psychological, unconscious, "subterranean" nature of any plan, the "subterranean urges" behind any design and any architecture, which is of course a vivid and poetically powerful metaphor for human behavior, guided by latent, irresistible basic forces, as he believed.

Finally, this exhibition was based on the idea of the poetic power of the "self-darkness" Dennis spoke about so often. We had our long, never finished discussions in his studio on Franklin Street in Tribeca, as well as in Catanzaro, in Rome, in Budapest, in Vienna, in Sarajevo and in Saint-Étienne. In these empathetic conversations, Dennis Oppenheim repeatedly spoke about the spontaneous and subconscious determinations of our actions and attitudes – irrational and uncontrollable, hysterical and chaotic – that he wanted to show in his work. He consequently refused the categories of conceptual art, land art, body art etc. and preferred instead very concrete, immediate interpretations of his work in the context of theater or performance. He regarded even his sculptural projects as a theater of improbabilities, as a scenography of uncertainties and freed imagination. In one of his brilliant essays, he sought to uncover his deepest motivation in the working process and found it in the irresistible desire of an "almost shamanistic immersion into self-darkness."

The metaphor of the shamanistic power of the artist, or that of the work of art, as an allegorical expression, and as code for the poetic competencies and linguistic specificities of contemporary art, reflects the real cathartic potentiality of the reception and interiorization of art. Instead of being pathetic – and somewhat naïve – we should consider this irrational, but evidently existing transmission of energies and emotions. The great masterpieces always teach us to understand their enigmatic power and exemplary status.

The acknowledgement of the power of this ungovernable and frightening "self-darkness" in different cultural contexts and symbolic forms, in myths and cults, in religious stories or in the ritual manipulations of black magic, in language or poetry determines the basic central narratives of the artists featured in the exhibition "Intriguing Uncertainties – Disturbing Narratives."

When Günter Brus and Hermann Nitsch from Central Europe, or their younger artist colleagues, like Sandra Vásquez de la Horra from Latin America, or Barthélémy Toguo from Africa, or Veronika Holcová, László László Révész and Nina Kovacheva from East-Central Europe, set free the latent potentiality of provocative and frightening imagination; when they try to represent ghosts and body transformations, black magic rituals and old fantasies of maledictions, religious topoi and psychoanalytical fixations on the body and pathology; when they work with never before seen combinations of images and words, they create a powerful and authentic narrative of "self-darkness," which is always and inevitably, profoundly and necessarily contextualized in the given real, historically determined cultural context.

When Jan Fabre elaborates his very special, unique, singular poetic universe on the basis of the old Flemish masters, 19th century Romanticism and modern Belgian cultural, religious, literary and artistic sensibilities, or when French artists Didier Trenet and Nicolas Dieterlé draw their psychotic and manneristic scenes with Antique, Hellenistic, High Renaissance and manneristic motifs and visual-sculptural topoi – which are entangled in strange, somewhat disturbing, but culturally absolutely familiar apocalyptic situations, historically well-known conflicts and theatrically articulated fights represented in woodcuts and miniatures of the late Middle Ages and Mannerism – they are operating within the mental realities of cultural heritage, of the traditions of art history, of ethical and philosophical conventions of the Occident, and in this way, they speak to our latent and hidden fears, the fantasies and phantoms that live deep under the fragile skin of modernity.

When Dennis Oppenheim created mechanical models of fatalistic and irreversible collisions and crashes of human "subterranean urges" and energies – negative, often destructive, yet intriguing and questioning – or sculptural materializations of the frightening shocks and bumps caused by the uncontrollable self-destructive forces of human nature, these invite us to follow their journey to the realms of excessive imagination, which is always based on very real, utterly concrete anthropological experiences. Their mechanics are full of life and death, emotions and movements, destructive and obscure motivations. When Jana Gunstheimer, László László Révész, Matt Bollinger, Muntean/Rosenblum, Iris Levasseur and Peter Seinturier create theater-like, dark spaces filled with human bodies, furniture, working instruments and artistic vehicles, which are kept in a strange, somewhat pathological uncertainty between the public sphere and the intimate, personal and hidden realms of individual life, they propose a scenography of obscurity and the state of indefinability. They all share a basic interest in theater, dance and performance, in the direct involvement of the body, which materializes the sensual and provocative imagery of the vital, powerful, complex psychological reality of being human. At the same time, this reality is evidently and inevitably contextualized in the ethnocultural, anthropological, historical constellations in which the real community, the real self in question lives, deals and works, communicates, thinks and dreams.

The exhibition "Intriguing Uncertainties – Disturbing Narratives" exclusively presents drawings by artists from Europe, North America, South America and Africa. Their artistic practice in the medium of drawing manifests a strong and profound engagement with the cultural heritage of previous historical periods, from the Middle Ages to late Symbolism, from Mannerism to Romanticism, from the Baroque era to Surrealism and Dadaism.

They all operate with strong, excessive images, with the presence of texts in the visual structure, with the poetic power of selected words within suggestive images, with cultural metaphors drawn from myths, religious subjects, collective memories, conventions and old, popular narratives, as well as with subconscious and pathological realms.

All the artists invited consequently ignore any tendency or demand for formalistic coherence of their work. They concentrate on the provocative and extreme intensity of revealing strong, unavoidable, elemental feelings that dominate and determine our attitudes and reactions. The accumulation of unplanned and ungovernable moments, the visualization of an "internal state of chaos" is at the center of their work. It is no paradox that while practicing an essentially rational methodology, they deal with irrational attitudes, and examine psychological, emotional and pathological realms. In communicating hidden, psychological states, in raising awareness of the inner "mental architecture," and in concretizing "dark processes," there is a confrontation between rationalistic methods and moments of mysterious enlightenment, intuitions and unconscious reactions. As Dennis Oppenheim explained: "I know it is a fantasy, that art is materialized by a combination of strong subterranean urges and a mysterious field of seduction that connects with primal forces, creating the urge to concretize and communicate. This is all an hysterical fantasy..."

(2016)

1. "Conversation between Germano Celant and Dennis Oppenheim," in: *Dennis Oppenheim. Venezia Contemporaneo*, Edizioni Charta, Milan 1997, p. 48.
2. Georg Simmel.
3. Hannah Arendt: "The Crisis in Culture," in: *Between Past and Future*, Penguin Books, New York 1977, p. 197.
4. "Conversation between Germano Celant and Dennis Oppenheim," in: op. cit, p. 52.
5. Edmund Burke: *A Philosophical Enquiry into the Origin of our Ideas of the Sublime and Beautiful*, edited with an introduction and notes by Adam Phillips, Oxford World's Classics, Oxford University Press Inc., New York 1990, p. 57.
6. "Essential Experiences – Time, Death, Radicality, Responsibility," exhibition curated by Lóránd Hegyi, Palazzo Riso, Palermo.
7. Emmanuel Levinas.
8. Edmund Burke: op. cit.
9. Ibid., p. 55.
10. Ibid., p. 57.
11. Ibid., p. 56.

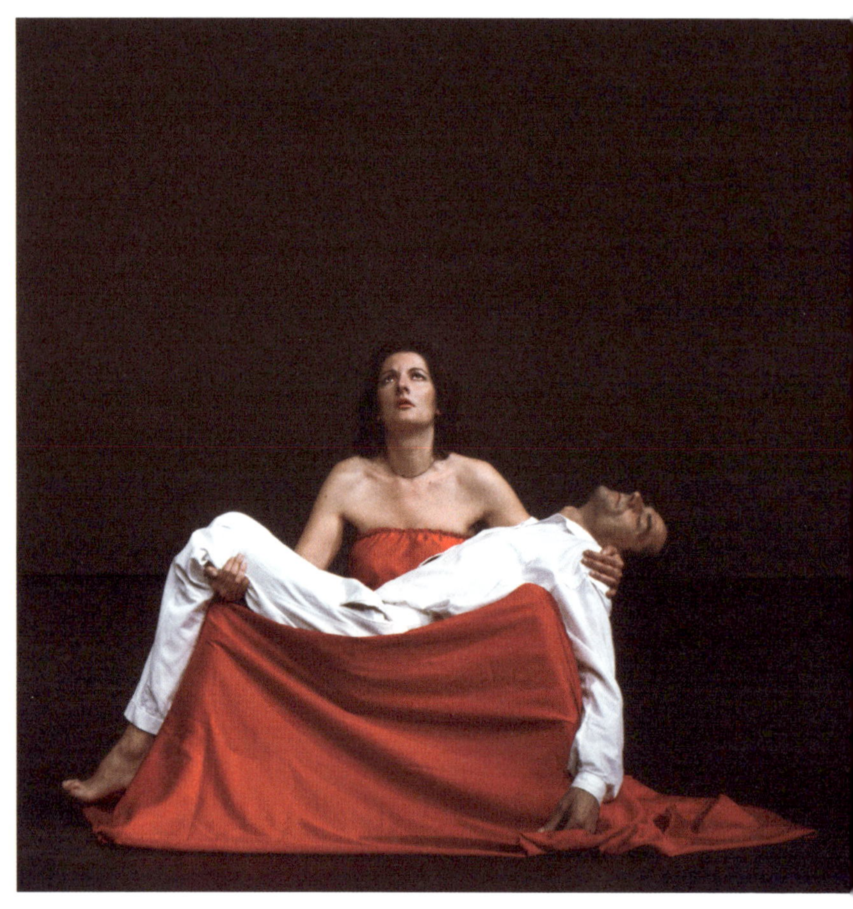

Marina Abramović
Pietà, 2002
Performance
Courtesy Collezione La Gaia, Busca

SPEAKING ARTISTS

Destiny – Vocation – Engagement – Language

"Art is the hieroglyph of potenza. This fact of being a hieroglyph in no sense impoverishes art: on the contrary, it exalts its ontological singularity to the extent that, if it is true that art is a higher act of imagination inasmuch as it accedes directly to being, it is so in a concentrated manner, strong and singular..."
(Antonio Negri, *Letter to Giorgio on the Sublime*)

"If you want to be a speaking artist, you have to be totally crazy, mad, extreme. Otherwise it doesn't work. You have to be a complete outsider, totally alone. If you are part of something, nothing will happen," Gilbert & George stated in an interview conducted by Martin Gayford.[1] What the artists thus expressed in a simple, clear and uncompromising way is nothing less than one of the most essential, significant, fundamental and central characteristics of artistic work, attitudes and positions: sovereignty, radical independence of any predefined judgments, methods or views – be they morally, politically, ideologically, socially or aesthetically binding – of any given community, system, social or cultural organization. What Gilbert & George are talking about is the peculiar special status of artists that enables – and, at the same time, compels – them to fulfill a specific vocation, namely to be able to consider and interpret human realities in a different way than non-artists, who do not have that language skill.

Gilbert & George speak of a specific language – an artistic language – and of the facility, capacity, power and magic of this specifically shaped, peculiarly structured, intentional, metaphorical and singular language, with which artists are able to touch, grasp and describe what is essential, real, unique, concrete, true and actual, with no regard for the social, moral, political, ideological, recorded and conventional hierarchies or emotional prescriptions and sociocultural obligations that usually determine everyday actions, functional connections and pragmatic communities of interest.

They consider it perfectly obvious that an artist can never be "part of something," in the sense of obligatory membership in a given sociocultural, intellectual or emotional community or organization in society. Quite to the contrary, artists always stand completely alone as a matter of principle; they must inevitably remain outsiders, and are often regarded as "crazy, mad, extreme" for that precise reason. Only this radical position far from conventional entrenchment, outside any morally, ideologically or aesthetically binding communities of values, unbound by determinative and compulsory values, far apart from predefined systems and hierarchies enables artists to find their own authentic, true and singular language. An artist has to be a "complete outsider" to achieve the capacity, energy and facility of radical language. An artist's visual language and capacity of expression depends on autonomy, sovereignty and independence. Language, or the capacity of speaking, is the essential, basic nature of art. As the artists put it so succinctly: "But art to us is a kind of visual language."[2]

This visual language differs from conventional, everyday, functional and pragmatic language, which refers to immediate and practical functions of everyday actions with specific purposes, by the metaphorical dimension that is inherent to it. The specific, intentional language of art is focused on a specific message, interpretation and communication, on the revelation of certain singular experiences made possible only by the radical nature of artistic engagement. This engagement is embodied in speaking, communication, and the development of the subversive capacity of language. And this language is meant to be read and understood.

"I think maybe that what we are trying to say we are doing is modern visual imagery. [...] They function like pictures, people read them

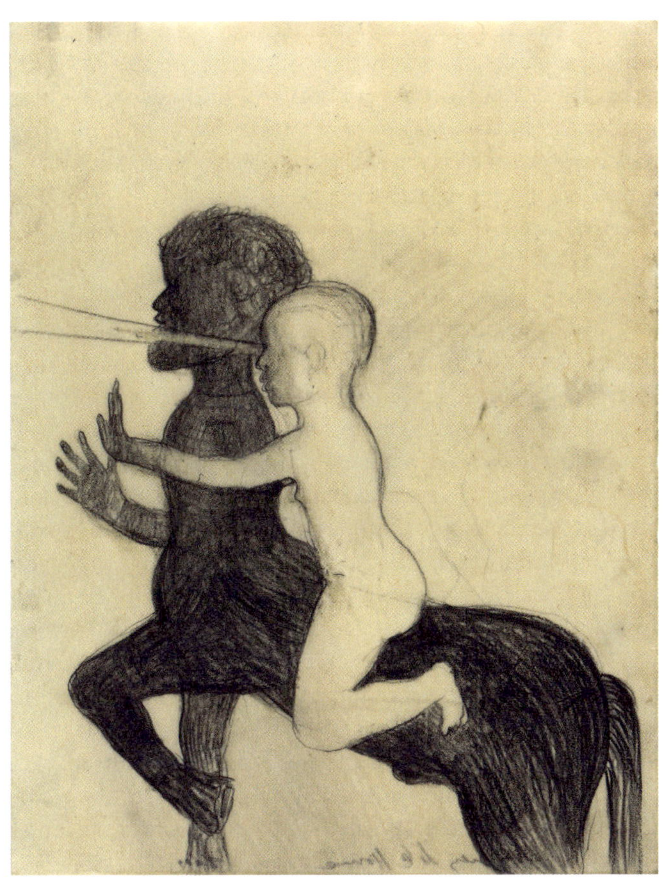

Sandra Vásquez de la Horra
El Centauro Y Yo, 2011
Pencil on paper, wax, 41 × 32.5 cm
Courtesy of the artist
Photo © the artist

like pictures, they speak as pictures, as art always has done. But they are up to date," Gilbert & George encapsulate their understanding of visual language, of a picture's peculiar capacity of expression.[3] The specific capacity of the artists, perpetually and consistently repeated, or rather the specific capacity of their works of art derives from language, from a peculiar, strange capacity of expression. Their pictures "speak as pictures, as art always has done." What this means – that the pictures speak – is that they communicate thoughts and emotions immediately and inexorably, in direct and suggestive, forceful and compelling ways, and that they are absolutely meant to be read and understood. This specific, intentional language is not just an essential peculiarity of art, but at the same time an ethical obligation: speaking is an imperative.

"*Narrare necesse est*: we humans must tell stories. That is the way it has always been and always will be. Because we humans are our stories, and stories must be told. Every human is 'the one that...;' and only stories ever tell who exactly we are. [...] If we give up storytelling, we give up ourselves," said German anthropologist Odo Marquard during a discussion in Weimar in 1999.[4] What he is talking about is the capacity of legitimation inherent in language, or in stories, which not only records an event, but uses language to create identities and realities. A new entity is reified in a story, a reality that receives its understandable, communicable and suggestive shape precisely from language. Language is the dense context of concretization, contextualization and reification of the anthropological, sociocultural and intellectual realities that determine our real, concrete situation. Artistic language possesses an extraordinary, hypersensual, suggestive and evocative nature that is reified in the metaphors of visual language.

For the specific, intentional, suggestive and evocative language of the artist to be understood, this language must be comprehensible, even self-evident. Comprehensibility is effective and immediate, forceful and seductive, charming and compelling, evocative, euphoric, self-explanatory and self-legitimating. This deep, firm and fundamentally ethical sense of duty and need for legitimation – which could even be called heroic, or passionate, romantic, emotional and dramatic – gives rise to a great challenge: "We want Our Art to speak across the barriers of knowledge directly to People about their life and not about their knowledge of art. [...] We want the most accessible form with which to create the most modern speaking visual pictures of our time."[5]

When Gilbert & George speak of the "most modern speaking visual pictures of our time," they emphasize the central significance of contemporary realities – modern, present, current and momentary – that their art intends to discuss and communicate, and they

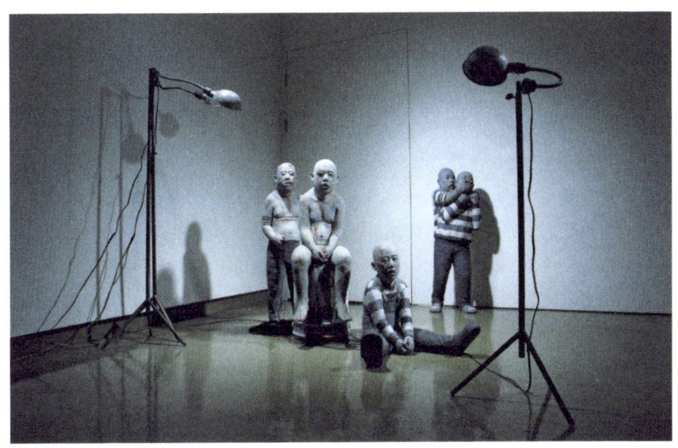

Sung Myung Chun
Swallowing the Shadow, 2007
Acrylic painting on fibre-reinforced plastic
Courtesy of the artist
Photo © D.R.

also reaffirm the aesthetic and ethical significance of immediacy, directness and comprehensibility, the necessary clarity of language. Creating the "most accessible form" is inextricably linked to a comprehensible, clear, understandable and effective description of contemporary realities, to the observation and communication of concrete, current, contemporary and momentary truths. The artists seek to use a comprehensible, contemporary, suggestive and evocative language to speak about actual current truths.

The aim of the "speaking artists" is to create a strong, complex, rich and true visual language that is expressive and evocative, suggestive and self-evident, radical and direct, and that directly communicates the real, complex and often contradictory integrity of anthropological constellations, the infinitely varied, multifaceted, complex yet banal, evident, ubiquitous, tangible and concrete manifestations of our anthropological and sociocultural realities. To them, language is the powerful and effective vehicle of this communication, the immediate reification of this revelation, and the means to describe contemporary realities, and thus an instrument of fundamental anthropological and cultural orientation in human life and in the universe.

The "most modern speaking visual pictures" are easy to recognize for any observer; their language is intended to be immediately grasped and understood by all people. The forceful, evocative, immediate and accessible language of art communicates contemporary life experiences, describes actual modern realities, and directly captures the manifestations of banal, present life. It is popular, so to say, because it is self-evident, effective, suggestive, strange and self-legitimating. This specific, highly concentrated, evocative and intentional language is a revelation of a direct approximation of everyday, tangible realities and life experiences; it is the language of radical directness.

An immediate, comprehensible, suggestive and modern visual language involves clear, deducible iconographic and psychological rules, and a teleological decisiveness that communicates modern, banal present-day narratives as almost "classical," rationally constructed and easily legible epics. These clearly structured contemporary epics reflect the unrestrained, limitless variety of human attitudes and conditions, and human relations within the complexity of entire sociocultural systems and ways of life, from political, ideological and religious symbols to commercial icons and logos, the colorful forms of the simulacra of consumer society. These contemporary epics operate with the specifically designed visual effectiveness of visual language. This specific language is simple, elemental, suggestive, dramatic and cool, and the decisive factor is always the permanent, fundamental discrepancy between popular legibility and evocative, enigmatic subversion.

"We want the most accessible modern form with which to create the most modern speaking visual pictures of our time," Gilbert & George write,[6] emphasizing the need for a suggestive, artistic message to be accessible and immediate. Two key elements are mentioned in this somewhat dramatic and romantic, ethically motivated statement: the creation of the "most accessible form," that is the visual creation of "speaking pictures," and the concept of modernity, the decisive presence of contemporary realities, of "our time," meaning the contemporary, everyday, directly witnessed experience of the present.

The "speaking pictures" communicate this utterly contemporary experience of life; they speak of our times, our lives, our immediate anthropological, psychological and cultural realities. There is no other essential experience but the contemporary and momentary experience of our very own present, immediate and personal lives. The historical dimensions of sociocultural systems and their representations are also considered, interpreted and captured as part of the anthropological complexity of individual contemporary realities. There is nothing but individual contemporary consciousness, determined by concrete, contemporary practices within the given structures of specific contemporary ways of life.

That is why "speaking artists," such as Orlan and Gilbert & George, Jan Fabre and Maurizio Nannucci, William Kentridge and Michelangelo Pistoletto, Braco Dimitrijevic' and Barthélémy Toguo, Miguel Angel Ríos and Marina Abramovic', Sandra Vásquez de la Horra and Gloria Friedmann, and many others, repeatedly emphasize the fundamental connection between "speaking visual pictures of our time" and the perception of the infinite integrity of anthropological realities, which are always naturally and necessarily structured and articulated in the various contemporary sociocultural, political and ideological situations and ways of life. It is an ethical imperative to "be completely modern," in the sense that "speaking artists" always and necessarily report on the realities of their time. The "speaking visual pictures of our time" communicate and reveal realities that are reified by the radical and subversive nature of the artist's specifically chosen, intentional, evocative, enigmatic yet extremely suggestive and accessible language.

This specific, intentional and evocative language unfolds in the context of a peculiar artistic concentration on what is fundamental, actual and essential, which is revealed in artistic statements with compelling and evident sensuality, irresistible directness, inevitable and startling obviousness, and poetic legitimacy. This poetic legitimacy creates strong, forceful metaphors in which our experiences and observations are concentrated. With forceful, irresistible suggestiveness and an enigmatic, evocative and complex aura, such self-legitimating metaphors speak of the most elemental and immediate life experiences, of the small and large, banal or emotional, grotesque or tragic, personal or public things that reify our relationships in infinitely varied anthropological constellations. Along these lines, Dennis Oppenheim has said, "I know it is a fantasy, that art is materialized by a combination of strong subterranean urges and a mysterious field of seduction that connects with primal forces, creating the urge to concretize and communicate. This is all an hysterical fantasy."[7]

As a "speaking artist," Dennis Oppenheim thus refers to the strong inner need to communicate, which is enabled precisely by a specific artistic language. The concretization of various subconscious experiences and emotional "subterranean urges" is immediately linked to communication about these experiences. "Speaking artists" work in the firm conviction that communication, speaking about their "subterranean urges," is at the center of their artistic work. The sensory concretization, the material and sensual reification of their experiences, only becomes possible in the context of a specific artistic language. This intentional, evocative and suggestive language is the actual terrain of artistic sensitivity, which makes possible the concretization of diverse experiences, and communication about observations that are otherwise incommunicable, without an artistic language or a specific context of hypersensitivity and concentration.

The metaphorical aspects communicated by the specific suggestive and intentional visual language of a work of art involve a peculiar intensity, concentration and essence, revealed in the context of artistic work. This peculiar intensity has a central significance, marked by ethical commitment, in the oeuvre of "speaking artists." Hannah Arendt speaks of a work of art's specific capacity to manifest "truth itself" with a clarity and transparency found nowhere else. The function of a work of art – otherwise devoid of purpose in a practical, tangible sense – consists in its manifestation of the consistency of the world in an absolutely clear way, so suggestive and brilliant that it opens up new perspectives on the perception of the world, new visions of reality. "And in this truth of consistency, the secularity of the world itself, which can never be absolute as such, as it is inhabited and used by mortals, appears, shines with a brilliance that also illuminates change and the course of things. What shines here is the consistency of the world, which, despite its relative permanence, never appears

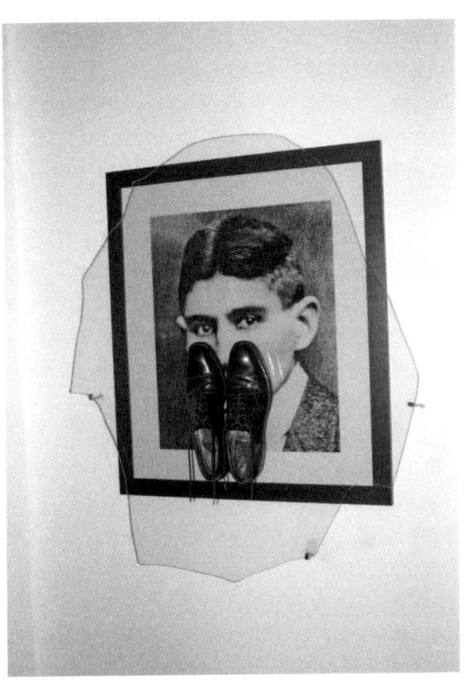

Braco Dimitrijević
Unwanted I (Kafka), 2006
Photography, glass, shoes, 71 × 61 cm
Courtesy of the artist
Photo © the artist

purely and clearly otherwise in the world of things; of truth itself, in which mortal humans find an immortal home. It is as if in the truth of the work of art, the secular permanence becomes transparent, revealing beneath it a glimpse of possible immortality."[8]

The beautiful metaphor of immortality refers to the peculiar capacity of a work of art to exhibit a specific intensity and concentration, and to manifest what is essential, fundamental and actual. Immortality is a state of integrity impossible in everyday life. If a work of art exhibits this metaphorical integrity in itself, it evokes a further horizon, a different, specific dimension from which we can observe and experience the given realities of life. Hannah Arendt speaks of the possibility of experiencing the consistency of the world, which cannot be captured in the world of things, or "truth itself," which cannot be grasped elsewhere, in a work of art and through a work of art. A work of art offers a unique, specific opportunity of perceiving an aspect of existence in a directly sensual way. A work of art's particular entity consists in its ability to communicate, by means of its specific, intentional language, a radically clear, transparent and poetically effective vision of the consistency of the world, otherwise hidden and concealed by the world of things. From this perspective, a work of art reifies a radical, fictional and imaginary integrity of existence, in which the alternatives of a life of immortality, which are practically impossible in the world of things, appear possible. This poetic, fictional and imaginary integrity refers to the alternative of an uncompromisingly essential and fundamental aspect that is practically impossible in the world of things. The experience, the perception of a glimpse of "possible immortality" through a work of art, involves an internalization of metaphorical integrity and the metaphor of a fictional, imaginary home.

This specific, fictional and imaginary home enables us to speak about experiences that cannot appear with the same intensity, sensual suggestiveness and provocative directness in the everyday world of things. When Jan Fabre speaks of the "Hour Blue," he refers to the specific capacity of art to use metaphorical language to communicate something that opens up, enriches and completes our tangible, practical everyday world through radical imagination and intensity, and enables us to rethink it subversively by means of fictional and imaginary perspectives, or the poetic perspectives of metamorphosis, transformation and change.

"Metamorphosis and hybridization have always been the poetic fulcrums of Fabre's work, a way of investigating rebirth and the transformation of the body in both spiritual and material terms. Hybridization and metamorphosis have always belonged to the human imagination as a vision of the world of otherness," writes Giacinto Di Pietrantonio about the capacity of artistic language as a carrier and reification of the artistic and ethical aspects of an artist's work.[9]

This second aspect of the special status of a work of art as hyperintense, suggestive communication of possible intellectual and anthropological perspectives, as a terrain of intense perception of the forms of transparency and clarity of essential experiences impossible in the world of things, refers to its most important function: to its capacity to reveal essential realities. Only this clarity and transparency enables mortal humans to find an "immortal home" where the things made by mortal hands outlast the death of their creators.

The specific capacity of works of art to reveal essential realities, and to hint at the perspectives of creative integrity and the transparency of the fundamental consistency of the world by perceiving these realities, enables humans to consider and contextualize their existence on a broader, more complex and intense, higher level through perception of a work of art. Works of arts offer humans the opportunity to grasp "the consistency of the world" and of "truth itself," which "never appears purely and clearly otherwise in the world of things," and to perceive "a glimpse of possible immortality" through this experience.[10] Works of art thus become a peculiar fictional and imaginary terrain, an island of "possible immortality," and it is precisely independence of the pragmatic rules of usefulness and practical, functional realities that makes possible a radical clarity and transparency.

In this context, immortality is a metaphor for the integrity of creativity and work, for the persistence of things made by humans. Immortality signifies an unlimited capacity of creation, an uncompromising radical nature of all possible intellectual and poetic constructs, an infinite creativity and freedom of imagination. A "glimpse of possible immortality" is revealed in works of art, which enables consideration of the existence and creative work of humans on a different, further horizon. This indication of a possible further horizon, of a different, special perspective, is the message of a work of art, and this is what sets it apart, as if an island, from the ordinary world of things.

The radical aspect that emerges from uncompromising, unlimited and intense concentration on the direct communication of fundamental realities creates a sensation of creativity, of an inexhaustible force capable of resisting human mortality. The optimistic, romantic metaphor of an "immortal home" refers to the ability and capacity of art to reify fundamental values in forms of art that are not clearly present in the world of things, that cannot be grasped as transparent and concentrated in the practical and utilitarian processes of ways of life.

This complex metaphor of immortality, which reinforces human immanence and affirms the creative integrity of artistic work, simultaneously refers to the specific entity of a work of art as a terrain for the revelation of fundamental experiences, and to its effect as communication of alternative perspectives, leading to new self-awareness. In this context, a parallel to Nietzsche's extremely complex metaphor of "living" can be discerned. The "living" metaphor also refers to radical integrity and an alternative way of considering the world, as Christoph Menke writes: "This program of a transformation of practice aims at a different way of doing. It is different from the model of action. 'Aesthetic transformation of practice' means: breaking the power of the concept of action (and all further related concepts: of purpose, of reasons, of intent, of capability, of self-awareness etc.) over the activity of doing. The lesson for artists is: we can be active in other ways than the purposeful, self-aware performance of practical capabilities. Nietzsche's term to describe this other way of doing, on this or the other side of action, is 'living.' Becoming active following the model of artists means not to act, but to 'live.'"[11]

The metaphor of "living" suggests a radical, uncompromisingly actualized integrity that emerges not in the context of purposeful actions with concrete, practical objectives, but in artistic doing. This emphasizes the special status, or the specific entity, of art as a terrain on which a sensually graspable, suggestive and infinite integrity can be actualized. This radical integrity, this independence of the rules and causalities of purposeful actions in the world of things, is possible only on the terrain of art, only in the doing of artists. "In artists' striving for integrity as an activity in ecstasy, however, it is not the acting subjects that actualize a purpose they know of and want; instead, artists active in ecstasy actualize – themselves: 'Humans in this state transform things until they reflect their power – until they are reflections of their integrity.' True, 'aesthetic activity and observation' may thus lead to a transformation, to the integrity of things. But this change that is caused is not executed in artistic activity: it is not the purpose of that activity. Artistic activity has no purpose that would serve as its foundation and orientation. Artistic activity is a 'reflection' or 'communication' of the state the artists experiences during this activity. [...] When Nietzsche describes it as 'ecstasy,' he means, as with the birth of tragedy, a state of 'enhanced forces and abundance,' which he again refers to here as 'Dionysian.'"[12] Similarly, Jan Fabre also speaks of the artist's state during his work as akin to ecstasy, as does Dennis Oppenheim when he proclaims the determination of his work by "subterranean forces."

Nietzsche introduces the concept of "forces" to explain the intensity and poetic concentration of works of art, and the fundamental difference between purposeful actions of a subject in the world of things, and purposeless artistic activity. He emphasizes the qualitative difference between useful objects and quasi-useless works of art. Purposelessness is linked to a claim to integrity, to unlimited, uncompromising creation, as purposeful action is necessarily limiting, as it is tied to fulfilling a previously known, deliberate and concrete function. The purposelessness of artistic activity positions works of art far from the world of things and enables radical activity, concentration and enhanced, infinite creative forces. "Nietzsche speaks of 'forces,' on the other hand, with respect to activities on the other side (or this side) of consciousness; forces are unconscious. That is precisely what the concept of ecstasy means: ecstasy is a state in which the subject's forces are enhanced to such a degree that they escape conscious control. Or conversely: the unleashing of forces while in ecstasy consists precisely in their transcending the aggregate state of conscious capabilities for purposeful action. That is why humans in a state of ecstatically enhanced forces are defined by an essential inability: 'the inability not to react (similar to certain hysterics who will take on any role at the slightest suggestion);' the inability of acting capacity as the force that compels aesthetic reaction and self-expression."[13]

Precisely this compulsion for self-expression is the mission and vocation of "speaking artists;" it is exactly what Dennis Oppenheim describes as the "urge to concretize and communicate." This mission that compels self-expression creates a specific sensitivity and sovereignty, a radical and unlimited urge to become active beyond purposeful actions; to exercise boundlessness, so to speak, and to reveal alternative ideas that refuse to accept the limitations of purposeful objectives. It is in this specific state – on the terrain of art, the island of artists – that a hyperintense evolution towards artistic integrity happens, without limits or narrow purposeful objectives, be they practical, political, didactic or moral.

This radical evolution towards integrity can be grasped in the context of artistic language, and in the practice of "speaking artists," and this intense experience suggests alternative perspectives and further horizons that reveal a different way of "living" in the Nietzschean sense. The experience is radical and intense, which is at the center of the engagement of "speaking artists." Obsession and a radical approach force Orlan to pursue hybridization; there is an obsessive approach to the theatrical rituals of dangerous self-destruction of the modern society of spectacles in the artistic practice of Miguel Angel Ríos and Bernardí Roig; there is Gloria Friedmann's subversive irony in referential gesticulations in a dense cultural and historical context; Michelangelo Pistoletto raises the power of language to absurdity, with the materialization of all political, historical and social connotations actually giving rise to an environment; Braco Dimitrijevic"s suggestive, sensual and immediately effective installations subversively reinterpret the hyperradical language of various modern political and cultural systems of manipulation: all these are examples of the deep and genuine engagement of "speaking artists" in reintegrating, rethinking and raising awareness of artistic practice from the perspective of the evocative, suggestive power of visual language, and from the perspective of language, communication, messages and perception of contemporary human, cultural, social and ideological realities.

In this context, Christoph Menke writes, "The fundamental trait of the aesthetic transformation of practice thus consists in learning to discern a conceptual distinction in the artist's model: learning to distinguish between acting and living in the realm of doing. The first result of this newly acquired ability to distinguish is a new description of the realm of practice. Once we have learned from artists that there is activity above and beyond action, we see how practicality seeps into life everywhere, bottom-up and top-down [...]. As a result of this new aesthetic description, 'living'

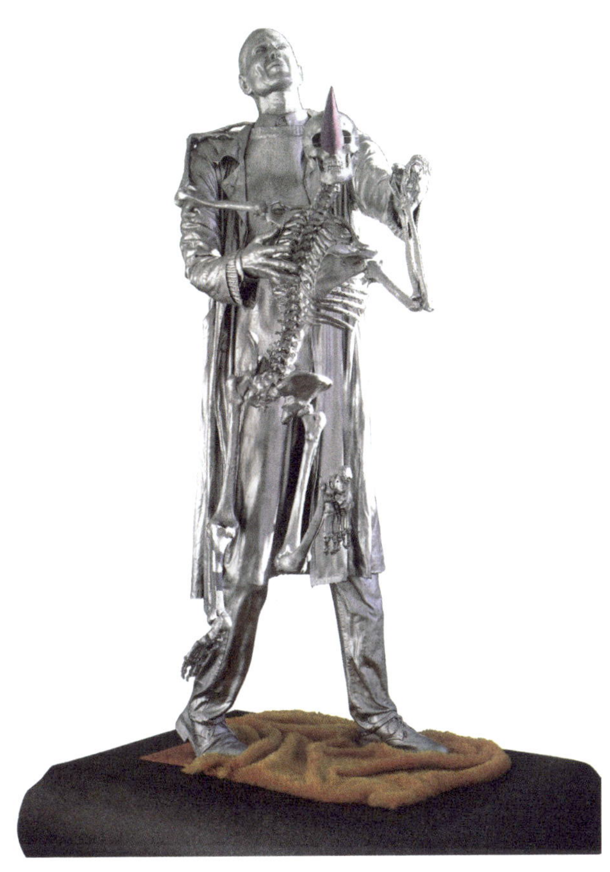

Gloria Friedmann
Le Gigolo, 2009
Metal, polyester, aluminium,
202 × 100 × 100 cm
Courtesy of the artist

is both the lowest (most elemental, descriptively speaking) and the highest (most challenging, normatively speaking) concept of a philosophy of practicality: 'living' is the determination of *movement* and of what is *good*."[14]

Such true "living" is revealed by the enhanced "forces" of ecstasy, by radical, extreme and completely unlimited artistic activity; and radical imagination, liberation from any purposeful, practical or limited objectives, and the unfolding of figures and narratives of improbability lead to an intensification of fundamental experiences. This is why Gilbert & George say, "If you want to be a speaking artist, you have to be totally, crazy, mad, extreme. Otherwise it doesn't work. You have to be a complete outsider, totally alone. If you are part of something, nothing will happen."[15] Craziness, madness and delirium, an extreme and radical approach, are elements of ecstasy that enable artists to virtually step outside the rules of normalcy, of the pragmatic world of things and of purposeful action. This extreme and radical nature of excesses and extravagance, set in a cultural and historical context, and such sensory, mental and emotional exaggerations and ideological, political and intellectual explosions, mark the works of Jan Fabre, Marina Abramovic', Miguel Angel Ríos, Andrei Molodkin, Oleg Kulik and Orlan.

Through this radical approach, artists achieve a special status that enables unrestrained, uncompromising, radical, unlimited and sovereign language and creation – though not accepted always and everywhere by everyone, by the entire community and cultural environment, without conditions or objections. Such free, concentrated and completely sovereign language focuses on the fundamental and essential aspects, though they may seem to manifest in the most insignificant, imperceptible and inconspicuous banalities and their observation. Gilbert & George's term "speaking artist" refers to this radical act of speaking, of saying something; to the fundamental vocation of artists to say something important, crucial, fundamental and essential. Nietzsche's metaphors of "living" and "ecstasy," Hannah Arendt's "truth itself" and Gilbert & George's "speaking artist" all indicate the ability and capacity of artistic activity to create an extremely concentrated, radically intensified, unrestrained and uncompromisingly unfiltered state of extreme sensitivity. If artists are bound to some action, if they are "part of something," if they are not complete outsiders, they cannot achieve this state of absolute sovereignty, and thus cannot be "speaking artists." Only the position as an outsider enables the radical and extreme sensitivity that allows artists to reveal a new entity by their doing.

Detachment and unfamiliarity, exterritoriality and extremes, intensity and radicalism, otherness and "being the odd one out" define adventure, which – according to Georg Simmel – has many things in common with works of art: "Precisely where continuity with life is rejected on principle, or does not even have to be unlearned because we are other, untouchable, the odd one out from the outset – that is where we speak of adventure. Adventure lacks the mutual pervasion of neighboring aspects of life that makes the latter whole. It is like an island in life that determines its beginning and end in accordance with its own formative forces and not, like part of a continent, based on the boundaries of what lies to its sides. [...] it is, after all, the nature of a work of art that it cuts out a piece from the endlessly continuous series of presentation and experience, detaches it from all connections to this side or the other, and gives it a self-sufficient shape, as if determined and bound together by an inner core. That a part of existence that is interwoven with its discontinuity should nevertheless be perceived as whole, as a coherent entity – that is the form that works of art and adventures have in common."[16]

Adventure: another complex, poetically dense, powerful and effective metaphor for the creative capacity of artists to create a separate form of existence "determined by the impulse of a life formed from within" that is extremely intense and sovereign, and exists "outside any continuity of life."[17] Georg Simmel's "adventure" metaphor describes the special status of artistic activity, and the specific entity of works of art, which finds "its center in a meaning existing unto itself" precisely through provocative independence and an extreme state of "being the odd one out;" through a radical "detachment from the convolutions and concatenations of those contents."[18]

Extreme, unbound exterritoriality stands "outside any continuity of life" and cannot be integrated into the pragmatic causalities of the world of things; it breaks away from the continuity and logic of life, and embraces integrity and radical intensity by doing so. Through uncompromising independence and "detachment from the convolutions and concatenations," adventures and works of art are "perceived, with all the one-sidedness and randomness of their contents, as if somehow all of life was contained and exhausted in each of them. And this seems to happen not less well, but more integrally because works of art in general stand outside life as a reality, and adventures in general stand outside life as an uninterrupted process that comprehensibly interweaves each element with its neighbor. Precisely because works of art and adventures are set apart from life [...] both are analog to the totality of life itself."[19]

This is the reason for the enigmatic, undeniable and powerful effect of works of art: the concentrated experience of a feeling of totality, the dramatic encounter with a hyperintense, concentrated totality of life, which can be grasped in the form of extreme unfamiliarity, of unusual, eccentric detachment. On this exterritorial island of peculiarities, on this terrain of improbabilities, which "lacks the mutual pervasion of neighboring aspects of life,"[20] we experience the sensation of an extremely intense integrity and evolution towards integrity of different spheres of life and experience. Exterritoriality, detachment, breaking away from the rational context of life, or – in Nietzsche's words – the purposeless act of artistic activities, and the purposelessness of works of art, as well as extreme, crazy and uncompromising existence as an outsider: all these lead to radical loneliness as the price paid for freedom and independence by "speaking artists."

Despite their close sociocultural and human ties, artists are fundamentally alone and solitary in their ultimate decisions; they seek methods to intensify their specific, evocative language so as to effectively communicate their message. When Michelangelo Pistoletto creates a material, sensual environment around the word HUNGER, he reifies the intellectual, intelligible and psychological connotations of a word, a concept and therefore a powerful, essential, defining and formative experience in this objective, tangible and material reality. He materializes the immaterial, and translates the intelligible into objective, material and sensual realities. By this, not only does the concept become an experience, but intellectual abstraction and generalization become psychological, emotional and anthropological realities, and singular, evocative, sensual and real manifestations of the human practice of life. The metaphor creates a tangible, material reality that can be experienced, and that communicates the message with physical, pragmatic and material directness. Like adventurers, artists "muster a central sense of life that winds through the eccentric-ity of adventure, and produces a new, meaningful necessity of life precisely because of the vast distance between the coincidental content given from the outside and the center of existence that gives cohesion and meaning."[21] The extreme intensity, evocative suggestiveness, enigmatic complexity and provocative, subversive sensuality of language reifies the metaphor of the "meaningful necessity of life" that "speaking artists" seek to communicate through their commitment and passion.

(2012)

1. Gilbert & George in an interview conducted by Martin Gayford, in: *Gilbert & George*, catalogue of the Musée d'Art Moderne de la Ville de Paris, October 1997-January 1998, Paris Musées 1997, p. 94.
2. Gilbert & George in an interview conducted by Martin Gayford, in: op. cit, p. 92.
3. Gilbert & George in an interview conducted by Martin Gayford, in: op. cit, p. 92.
4. Odo Marquard: "Narrare necesse est," in: *Odo Marquard, Philosophie des Stattdessen. Studien*, Philipp Reclam jun., Stuttgart 2000, p. 60.
5. Gilbert & George: "What Our Art Means," in: *The Words of Gilbert & George. With Portraits of the Artists from 1968 to 1997*, Thames and Hudson in association with Violette Editions, London 1997, p. 149.
6. Ibid., p. 149.
7. Dennis Oppenheim: "Conversation Between Germano Celant and Dennis Oppenheim," in: *Dennis Oppenheim. Venezia Contemporaneo*, Edizioni Charta, Milan 1997, p. 48.
8. Hannah Arendt: *Vita activa oder Vom tätigen Leben*, Piper Verlag GmbH, Munich 1967, p. 202 (own translation).
9. Giacinto Di Pietrantonio: "In Form," in: *Jan Fabre: The Years of the Hour Blue*, exhibition catalogue, Musée d'Art Moderne de Saint-Étienne Métropole, Silvana Editoriale, Cinisello Balsamo 2012, p. 144.
10. Hannah Arendt: op. cit., p. 202.
11. Christoph Menke: *Kraft. Ein Grundbegriff ästhetischer Anthropologie*, Suhrkamp Verlag, Frankfurt am Main 2008, p. 114 (own translation).
12. Ibid., p. 112 (own translation).
13. Ibid., p. 113 (own translation).
14. Ibid., p. 114 (own translation).
15. Gilbert & George in an interview conducted by Martin Gayford, in: op. cit., p. 94.
16. Georg Simmel: "Das Abenteuer," in: Georg Simmel, *Das Abenteuer und andere Essays*, Fischer Taschenbuch Verlag, Frankfurt am Main 2010, p. 41 (own translation).
17. Ibid., p. 39 (own translation).
18. Ibid., p. 40 (own translation).
19. Ibid., p. 41 (own translation).
20. Ibid., p. 41 (own translation).
21. Ibid., p. 43 (own translation).

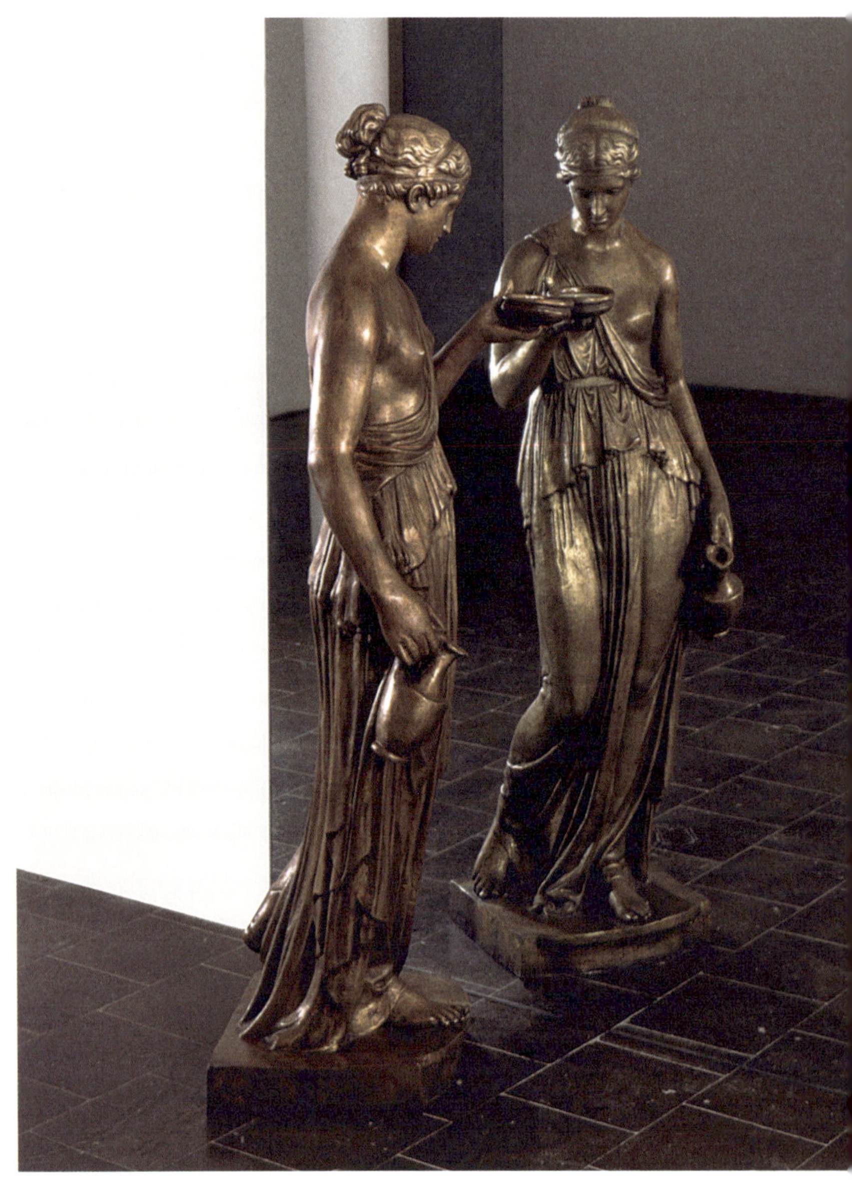

Michelangelo Pistoletto
Il dono di Mercurio allo specchio, 1971
Mirror, bronze, variable dimensions
Courtesy Cittadellarte - Fondazione Pistoletto, Biella

THE GIVING PERSON

The Gesture of Giving in the Absence of an Addressee

"We no longer have recourse to the grand narratives – we can resort neither to the dialectic of Spirit, nor even to the emancipation of humanity as a validation for postmodern scientific discourse.
But as we have just seen, the little narrative (*petit récit*) remains the quintessential form of imaginative invention..."
(Jean-François Lyotard, *The Postmodern Condition: A Report on Knowledge*)

How wonderfully simple, straightforward, modest, and unpretentious is the language Gilbert & George use to describe one of the greatest, most enigmatic, and most powerful abilities of art – the generosity of giving, offering, donating, and contributing: "Civilisation has always depended for advancement on the 'giving person.' We want to spill our blood, brains, and seed in our life-search for new meanings and purpose to give to life."[1]

The "giving person" is the real creator of values, the actual author of all stories, the courageous and indefatigable messenger, the charismatic hero of the long journey of life, the compelling and inexhaustible power of civilization. The "giving person" proffers something that we can perceive and accept, that we really need, use, and internalize.

But what is even more paradigmatic in Gilbert & George's essay *What Our Art Means* is the rich, complex, and expanded context in which they talk about the decisive act of giving, offering, and sharing. On the one hand, they write about civilization, i.e. history, collective experiences, memories, tradition, and innovation, or, as they put it "good traditions and necessary changes," as well as about the universal values of good and evil: "We want to find and accept all the good and bad in ourselves."[2] On the other hand, they connect the act of giving to a never-ending search for "new meanings and purpose to give to life."

Both motifs deepen, expand, and specify the gesture of giving and enrich the ethical, philosophical, and aesthetic context of contributing. These additional referential elements give rise to a multi-faceted new context in which giving may be interpreted as mutual, interactive, discursive, and creative. The act of giving and offering becomes a central category which elicits moral and aesthetic questions.

Since artists harness their entire life, their power, their body, and their intellect – "our blood and brains" – to a maximum extent, unconditionally, and relentlessly, the act of giving is invested with a dramatic dimension and a radicalness which bears some similarity to Lyotard's notion of enthusiasm. Artists allow us to perceive and acknowledge "all the good and bad" in human beings in order to comprehend the totality of life, while they are looking for "new meanings and purpose to give to life."

The first task to "find and accept all the good and bad in ourselves" involves an heroic and, at the same time, dangerous juxtaposition of antagonistic moments, based on, and legitimized by, an understanding of human totality, with artists accepting the moral consequences of evil as an act of self-sacrifice that has almost sacral connotations. They take on evil, they willingly receive moral rejection and negative judgments in order to demonstrate the "bad side" of humanity, and manifest the totality of human existence with all negative and positive realities. They play the role of negativity in the interest of a positive claim to totality, and this possibly somewhat concealed ethical vocation legitimizes their choices.

The second task, this "life-search for new meanings and purpose," presupposes an open and enthusiastic attitude that mingles ethical, aesthetic, as well as utopian and pragmatic aspects.

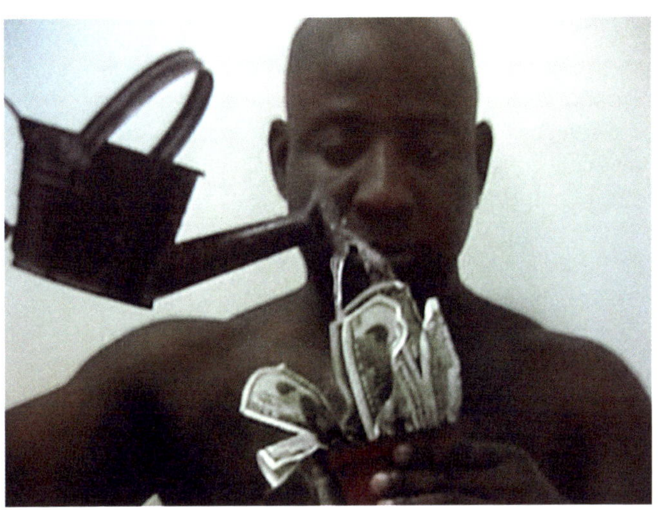

Barthélémy Toguo
Head Above Water III, 2005
Mixed media
Courtesy of the artist
Photo © the artist

The "life-search for new meanings and purpose" is presented as an ethical commitment, a calling, a choice artists have made for themselves; what is new may indirectly be construed as something better. Artists are looking for what is new because they believe in what is better; what is new makes them hope that they can find what is better. This on-going search is inspired by hope, and hence it is both legitimate and meaningful. This search becomes a calling, a commitment, the artists' main task, and the focal point of artistic activity. It is not curiosity or a naïve and evolutionist conviction which acts as a driving force; rather, it is the artists' endeavor to find – and give – something better. The act of giving and of sharing is the ultimate goal which is pursued during this never-ending search, during this long journey.

The maximalist claim to totality does not differentiate between good and bad, or between good and better, as it wants to comprehend and display everything. The ethical imperative, the choice one has made, the enthusiastic search for what is new evokes visions of a better reality that artists want to find and show to other

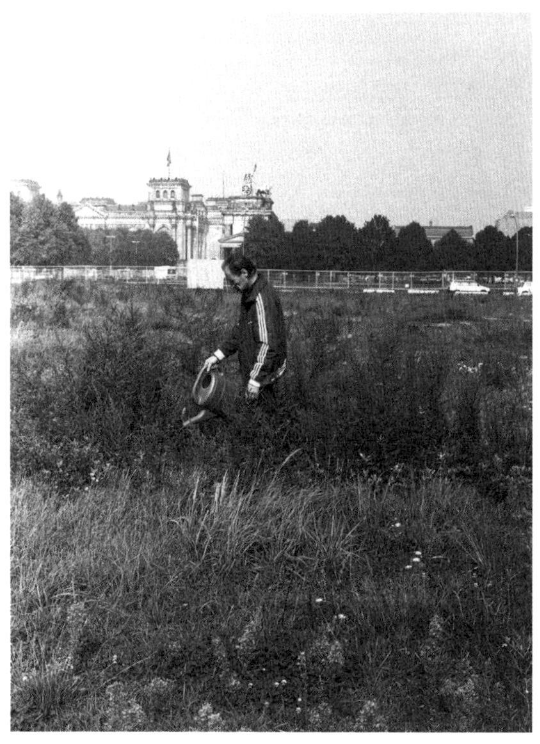

Lois Weinberger
Brandenburger Tor, 1994
Black and white photography
Courtesy of the artist
Photo © the artist

people. This is a huge and ethically legitimized emotional calling – finding what is new and giving it to fellow human beings. The act of giving is invested with the connotation of making a sacrifice and of acting as a visionary, a prophet, a Messiah; in either case, the ethical and aesthetic discourses assert claims to each other.

In the first case the artists' proposal, i.e. the subject of giving, is the bold, anarchic, and maximalist claim to totality that ignores the moral borders between good and bad, as well as its outcome, the total vision of human reality; in the second case, in contrast, giving is represented by the enthusiastic search for what is new. In either case enthusiasm dominates artistic practice.

In his interpretation of Lyotard, Walter Reese-Schäfer states the following: "Enthusiasm is an aesthetic emotion... Enthusiasm ranks among sublime feelings and as such it is 'shapeless and amorphous.' In this condition the danger of committing an error is enormous."[3] It is at the same time amoral, cathartic, anarchic, and creative. "Nevertheless, enthusiastic ardor, in its temporary vehemence, preserves ethical validity, it is an energetic emblem, a tensor of 'wishing.'"[4]

Gilbert & George touch upon sensitive, complex, and contradictory issues. The liberating, anarchic, and creative claim to totality, the enthusiasm "of the whole" – "We want to respect and honour 'the whole,'"[5] as they put it – blurs the borders between positive and negative phenomena and intentions, or negates the act of passing a moral judgment on the presentation of "the whole." The ethical lies in the commitment to an unpretentious presentation of reality, in an uncompromising way of facing reality, in the anarchic and liberating gesture of flying in the face of existing social and moral conventions.

This is not about a soothing kind of philanthropy or about charity, you don't just give certain useless and superfluous things of which you have plenty. You don't just give nice little gifts or simple leftovers, but you offer what is most elementary and existential. In the context of enthusiasm, which harbors a liberating and creative potential, which is characterized by "an energetic emblem," and which is imbued with a certain vagueness, giving becomes the artists' key ethical commitment. Walter Reese-Schäfer comments on this as follows: "This vagueness ensures that there is no defined notion on which one would have to agree; however, there is, at the reflective level, the capacity to comprehend, delineate, and present."[6]

This cathartic and creative vagueness implies boundlessness, a positive, pluralistic, and anti-hierarchic claim to totality, but also the unlimited and undefined nature of the perception of totality which lies at the heart of a "giving person"'s endeavors. These persons give although they don't know exactly who the recipient is. They give although they don't know exactly if their gift, their offer, or their proposal is accepted. They give without any moral consideration of selective categories and decisions. Their enthusiasm is ultimately subversive and, as such, liberating. Giving therefore becomes a crucial commitment. Giving is specified as the source of all creative activities and preoccupations. Giving is defined as an objective and as the search for the new meaning of life.

Like a source from which water gushes forth generously, inexhaustibly, and powerfully, artists offer their visions and emotions, their suggestions and their utopias, their joy, their ardor, their doubts, and their sorrows. This fresh and clear water may be used reasonably, economically, carefully, productively, or, in contrast, stupidly, irresponsibly, and even destructively and cynically. Likewise, the act of giving – the artists' gift – may be received openly, sensibly, thankfully, collaboratively, and constructively, or disapprovingly, arrogantly, uncooperatively, and destructively. The fresh water from the source is elementary and essential as it produces new life. We may drink it, we may use it to irrigate the dry soil, to help plants grow, to cook, to put out a fire, to quench a suffering person's thirst and thereby save his or her life; but we may also squander it irresponsibly, abuse it, or employ it destructively.

The same goes for giving artists. We may perceive the message of their act, ponder it, take it seriously, internalize it, and deal with it critically and analytically, or we may neglect, ignore, misunderstand, or even deliberately misinterpret it, use it for destructive purposes, manipulate, or abuse it. In this process artists are at the recipient's mercy because they never know for sure who hears their voice when, how, and where; they never know for sure who receives and acknowledges their message, who accepts or rejects their gift, who understands or misunderstands their suggestions, who shares their experiences, who opposes the idea of this community, who takes up or declines their offer to talk and to reflect on something together, who regards their message as an opportunity for participation, a gesture of empathy, or who abstains from any communication and from any encounter. The likelihood of perception depends on the recipient; artists are "giving persons" who, as a rule, have little immediate influence on how their message is perceived, and ignore how their work will fare. Artists are, in a way, naked and unprotected in this interaction, and they don't even know whether an interaction takes place at all. Their generosity means that they continue to give willingly – despite this uncertainty, their munificence knows no bounds.

But there is another, and equally significant, moment of uncertainty – the crisis of universal legitimacy of the object that is given. Artists are not just irritated by the uncertainty associated with their giving and the unknown fate of their gift, but also because of the justification, assessment, and contextualization of the act of giving itself. They have no unambiguous, unconditional, universal, and external explanations for entities and values, they cannot refer to an ubiquitous system of values, they cannot expect the persons and communities who receive what they give to speak the same language as they do, they cannot expect these people to interpret their message in its original meaning, and to share their values and ideologies. Artists don't know who they give their work to, and they have no clear ethical basis that would legitimize their choice and methodology. The object that is given also lacks an external explanation such as language, method, or orientation. There are no grand, comprehensive, and universal narrativities to explain and autonomize the object and purpose of giving unconditionally, universally and fundamentally.

Artists cannot work on the basis of external explanations or a universally valid, irrefutable common sense, or *sensus communis*. There is no universal, conventional *sensus communis*; it is the artists' job to create an occasional *sensus communis* in an intermittent, temporary, dissolving, and for ever reconstituting community. The legitimacy of giving and perceiving their gesture is as intermittent and temporary as the object and act of giving. The content and orientation of giving is only legitimized internally. Only specific immanent conditions and the intermittent, ephemeral, specifically determined, hic et nunc conditioned, and not generalizable real constellation of existing common connections create a concrete, real, temporarily valid basis for the perception of giving. Michael Newman calls this the "specific contextual or situational meaning of the elements and the work of art" which may activate its references in specific, individual, and real communities.[7] This "specific contextual or situational meaning" reflects concrete, temporary, and for ever reconstituting common realities; universal, external, abstract, and ethical narrativities are not relevant.

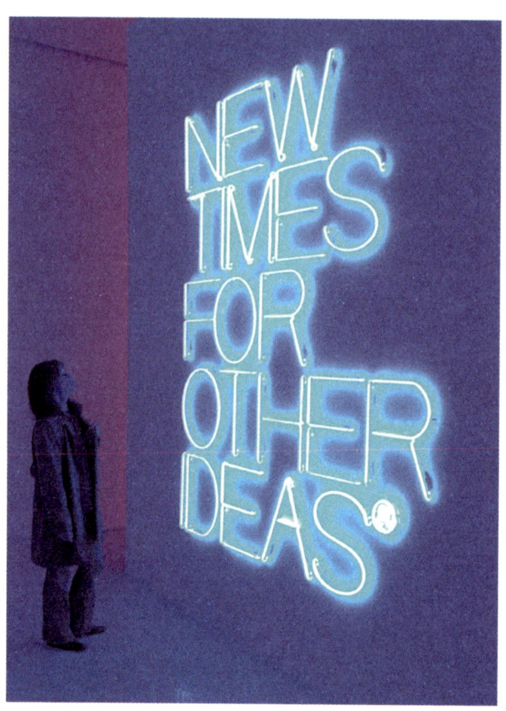

Maurizio Nannucci
New Times for Other Ideas, 2005
Neon on wall, variable dimensions
Fondazione delle Arti
Photo © Solares

Thus, artists who give are left entirely to their own devices since they can expect no shared basis, no universal legitimacy, no grand, comprehensive, unconditional, and common narrativities. Their giving is the purpose of their work, but they have no universally valid, ubiquitous, and unconditional communication built on a *sensus communis*, not even ethical comprehension. Gilbert & George write about the necessity of solitude, extremity, and insanity because the obsessive decision to give something important causes radical solitude and extreme distance. Artists, i.e. giving persons, are utterly alone, not just because they don't know the receiving person but also – when taking a decision on the object and language, on common relevance and micro-communication, on contextual

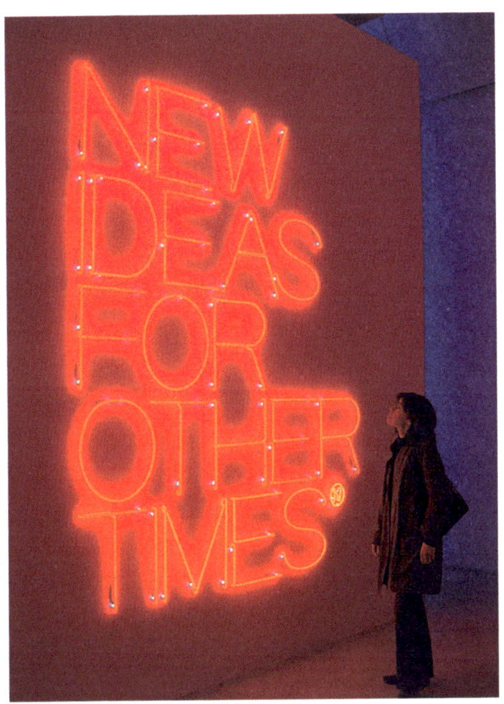

Maurizio Nannucci
New Ideas for Other Times, 2006
Neon on wall, variable dimensions
Fondazione delle Arti
Photo © Solares

meaning – because they can't resort to external narrativities and universal explanations.

By referring to the example of contemporary architecture, Lyotard explains the absence of a "universal addressee" to receive the gift: "People don't build simply in order to put a roof over their heads, they build in order to render a homage. The act of building is an act of honour rendered, and the tragedy is that of knowing who or what is the addressee of this gift. The great architectures of the past knew to whom buildings should be addressed. It could be a divinity, in all forms; it could be a prince; it could be an Idea of Reason, such as the Republic, or the People, or the Proletariat, as in certain aspects of the

Modern movement. But it was always the universal addressee. Today we don't know the destination of building, and this too is an aspect of the failure of the universal."[8]

Facing the radical absence of a "universal addressee," artists have to decide on a case-by-case basis, when dealing with a specific constellation, on the subject, the addressee, and the mode as there are no conventional, generally valid narratives which can be taken for granted and determine their actions: "The grand narrative has lost its credibility, regardless of what mode of unification it uses, regardless of whether it is a speculative narrative or a narrative of emancipation." Lyotard clearly points out that "grand narratives" always present a unified, homogenous, and universally valid system which determines methodology and objectives just as much as the relations between individuals and common legitimacy.[9] The loss of legitimacy of "grand narratives" also involves a "dissensus within pluralism," as stressed by Andrew Benjamin: "it is already clear that the conflict that marks the debate concerning the presence or absence of what Kristeva called 'transcendent truth,' or what Lyotard calls 'grand narrativities,' can only be understood and accounted for in terms of a theory of dissensus; one which recognizes the absence of a final resolution. In other words justice can only be done to dissensus within pluralism."[10]

Lyotard uses radical language when talking about the impossibility of consensus, or when expounding on the possibility of "paralogy," rather than illusionary universalism, based on consensus: "Consensus is only a particular state of discussion, not its end. Its end, on the contrary, is paralogy. This double observation (the heterogeneity of the rules and the search for dissent) destroys a belief that still underlies Habermas's research, namely that humanity as a collective (universal) subject seeks its common emancipation through the regularisation of the 'moves' permitted in all language games and that the legitimacy of any statement resides in its contributing to that emancipation... A recognition of the heteromorphous nature of language games is a first step in that direction."[11]

The radical absence of consensus, the de-legitimizing of "grand narratives" constitutes a challenge to formulate immediate, sensitive, and artistic answers which reflect specific constellations and require no external universalistic legitimacy, but act in concrete, real, individual situations – an attitude, in other words, which positions itself within immanent relations. This challenge results in a new, matter-of-fact, specific, gentle, non-didactic, non-paternalistic, non-Messianic, non-future-oriented, immediate responsibility, modesty, and empathy geared towards the real present situation.

Artists need to decide on a case-by-case basis, they need to specify the object of giving in real and concrete situations, they need to evoke a specific, real, and at least temporarily active community, they need to deploy their methods and pursue their strategies such that they are effective and relevant to the community. When referring to political action, Jean-François Lyotard writes about a "new ethical and civil responsibility" which only allows for "defensive and local comments." "That is what I would like to call 'new modesty.' Rather than totalizing universalism, Lyotard presents a 'new responsibility' which expects the downfall of universality, and thus addresses the mutual independence and even the mutual incompatibility of highly different responsibilities on a case-by-case basis with flexibility, tolerance, and 'agility.' In his dialog *Au juste*, Lyotard proposes a model for such decision-making – *phronesis*, Aristotle's practical wisdom, allowing him to pass a judgment in individual situations in which there is no overriding criterion" (Walter Reese-Schäfer).[12] This "new modesty," which invariably regards concrete and real constellations as well as existing, temporary, and shared situations as the points of departure of artistic work, views empathy, solidarity, participation, and reconciliation as the key ingredients of giving.

The personal stories of giving imbue this exhibition with a feeling of intimacy and involvement. Artists create new contexts, offer specific constellations of shared relevance and personal perspectives that include our own experiences, sensitize what is private, personal, internal, and intimate, and trigger our empathy.

This exhibition has been embedded in a sensitive and soft architecture featuring flexible, permeable walls; within its main areas interactions between neighboring artists are fostered. These areas describe public, collective, and shared competencies, as well as private, personal, and individual spheres. In the first area old and archaic topics are predominant, tales told by collective memory, reflections of myths and cults, connotations of various rites and meditations. In another area we find poetic and sensitive artistic statements referring to interpersonal micro-communication within immediate micro-communities, and revolving around personal, intimate, fragile, and frequently concealed micro-narratives. Along another exhibition axis war, destruction, fear, death, and mourning are contrasted with peace, harmony, tranquility, contemplation, and hope, with individual artworks alluding to cultural, historical, ethical, and aesthetic discourses.

Gilbert & George's work featuring the exposed, publicly exhibited, and disclosed naked body – a metaphor of self-sacrifice, devotion, dedication, surrender, as well as of unconditional giving and offering – is confronted with Jan Fabre's highly compelling floor installation. Its discarded and empty parts of armor and harness flung to the ground elicit painful memories of the absence of a living body, as well as the disappearance of life, the pointless haughtiness and glory of the warrior, the tragic condescension of the ruler, the blindness of the soldier who is convinced of the protection afforded by the tank and of imminent victory. Contrasting the naked, surrendered, self-sacrificing, unprotected body whose posture is unmistakably reminiscent of traditional depictions of Christ taken off the cross with empty, proud, and shining parts of armor which once shielded a strong warrior's body from harm but now serve as *memento mori* or *vanitas* symbols promotes interactions and testifies to the complexity of references.

A similar dialectic relationship emerges between the area occupied by Luigi Ontani and Maurizio Nannucci. In this case, oriental meditation, the quest for harmony, and a matching physical awareness are confronted with Western philosophy, analytical thought, and the paradigms of development and utopia.

Gianni Dessì's monumental and sublime white male figures – displaying an ambivalence which addresses classical art-historical conventions while challenging traditional modes of presentation – interact with Kiki Smith's tender, troubling, tormented and tormenting white female figures that convey pathological narratives. A key motif seems to be their enigmatic, inexplicable, agnostic, and culturally contradictory quality.

Ilya Kabakov's fears, his ancient and eternal distress, his anguish engendered by dependence, surrender, seclusion, restriction, immobility, escape, as well as a silent and stealthy disappearance – all of this is articulated by a closed room whose sad pictures remind viewers of another reality; its specious conviviality renders an escape even more futile. Opposite Kabakov's work, Jean-Michel Alberola writes his doubts and concerns on a wall, using both pictures and texts. These are something of a trap, as they make it impossible for us to unearth their true meaning, their causality and connections; on the other hand, they also act as an inescapable and violent whirlwind propelling viewers to unknown, dark places beyond their control, giving rise to arbitrary and absurd, but still quite conceivable connections between appearances and notions, experiences and memories. Their works are characterized by despair, agnosticism, distress, uneasiness, and anxiety, but also by curiosity, skeptical reason, and analytical obsession; their dialog adds new dimensions to their presentation.

The exhibition "THE GIVING PERSON" pays homage to artists who have the consistent, inexhaustible, non-theatrical, and silent courage to share with us their power, concentration, emotions, thoughts, commitment, obsessions, and experiences. They want to reach and affect us with their empathy even though they are not in a position to know the addressee.

(2005)

1. Gilbert & George: "What Our Art Means," in: *Gilbert & George*, catalogue, Musée d'Art Moderne de la Ville de Paris, Paris 1997, p. 362.
2. Ibid., p. 362.
3. Walter Reese-Schäfer: *Lyotard zur Einführung*, Junius Verlag, Hamburg 1988, p. 68.
4. Ibid., p. 68.
5. Gilbert & George: op. cit., p. 362.
6. Walter Reese-Schäfer: op. cit., p. 69.
7. Michael Newman: "Revising Modernism, Representing Postmodernism: Critical Discourses of the Visual Arts," in: *Postmodernism*, Lisa Appignanesi (ed.), Free Association Books, London 1989, p. 134.
8. Jean-François Lyotard: "Response to Kenneth Frampton," in: *Postmoderism*, op. cit., p. 91.
9. Jean-François Lyotard: *The Postmodern Condition: A Report on Knowledge*, Manchester University Press, Manchester 1984, p. 37.
10. Andrew Benjamin: *Art, Mimesis and the Avant-Garde – Aspects of a Philosophy of Difference*, Routledge, London & New York 1991, p. 135.
11. Jean-François Lyotard: op. cit., 1984, p. 65.
12. Walter Reese-Schäfer: op. cit., p. 54.

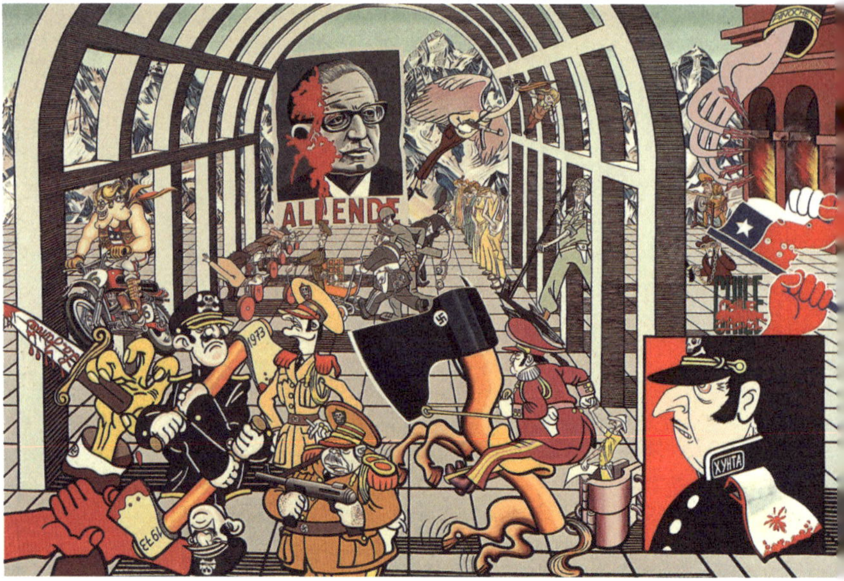

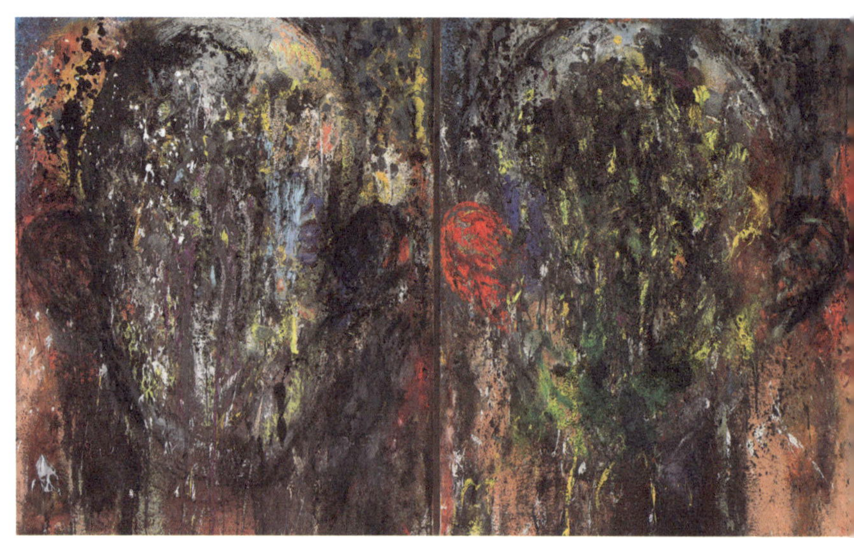

Erró
Allende, 1974
Glycerophtalic paint on canvas,
220 x 330 cm
Courtesy of the artist

Jim Dine
Four Ears, 2016
Oil on canvas, diptych, 139 x 226 cm
Courtesy Galerie Templon,
Paris and Bruxelles

TWO ROADS OF RE-VISITING THE NARRATIVES: ERRÓ AND JIM DINE

This essay tries to interrogate on the very specific concept of the narrative competence of painting and the metaphoric evocations connected with it in the oeuvres of two paradigmatic figures of the 1960s at both sides of the Atlantic, whose work has been often identified with tendencies of New Realism or Pop Art: the 1932 born Guðmundur Guðmundsson – later named Erró – from Iceland and the 1935 born James Lewis Dine – later named Jim Dine – from Cincinnati, Ohio. Their extremely rich and complex work seems to be re-visited in our days and reveals significant relevancies about the painterly narrative.

An interesting episode in their life: in 1963 the European painter Erró travelled on board of an ocean liner to the United States to discover the legendary New York art scene and to complete his narrative repertoire. Two years later the American artist Jim Dine travelled to Europe by ship to discover the Old Continent in order to find the narrative in the ancient art he was passionately looking for. For both artists these journeys were extremely significant to understand their own ways of dealing with subject matter.

For the European painter Erró the discovering of New York of the Age of Pop Art, the participation in the very vivid and exciting art life of the American metropolis, the friendship with Rosenquist, Rauschenberg and Wesselmann, the experience of the free atmosphere and the unlimited intensity of the spirit of artistic milieu of the post-war capital of Modernism enforced his aesthetic engagement in creating a profoundly contemporary narrative which could have been connected with the great tradition of narrative art from the Middle Age until Expressionism and Magical Realism and at the same time represents the fragmented, non-linear, de-constructed and eclectic story-telling of our age.

For the American artist Jim Dine the presence in the London art life, the active participation in the revolting Beat culture and in the freely experimenting literature, performance and music scene as well, as the immediate experience of the old – classic – European art, the re-visiting of the history of European painting enforced his convictions of the dramatic power of emotions in the art work and the credibility of narratives. More surprisingly, the seemingly paradoxical relation between radical Beat culture and historical tradition of visual arts reveals itself through the introduction of emotional engagement, which gives the explication of the importance of narratives. Both in his performances and musical praxis as well, as in his approaching to historical heritage of painting we can witness the search for authentic narratives, which are not at all obliged to be completely contemporary but which can include highly complex historical and cultural references, selected – of course – from the point of view of the contemporary narrator.

For both artists, the necessity of creating authentic narratives based on personal, cultural, historical experiences became a central moment of their artistic praxis. While the majority of their colleges de-legitimized – or at least ironically relativized – the narrative aspects of art works, Erró and Jim Dine emphasized the passionate personal comments and the relation between subjective experiences and the objective image. While their radically contemporary image-production seems to be part of the contemporary, familiar, banal world of indifferent and impersonal things, they fill actually the emptiness of the so-called objective world with subjective – that means: passionate, emotional, subjective – comments and references.

Although both artists were considered at the early 1960s as leading figures of the newly emerging urban Pop Art and both were presented in very important galleries like Sidney Janis Gallery in New York, or Galleria Arturo Schwarz in Milan, also at very significant group shows like "Environments – Situations – Spaces" at the Martha Jackson and David Anderson Galleries in New York, or "Involvement Show" at the March Gallery in New York, it became more and more clear that their approach to the narrative, the evocative poetical power of the connotations and associations and – specially in the case of Jim Dine – the hidden emotionality and sometimes even dramatic, autodestructive, passionate darkness – or the diabolic, excessive imagination in the painting of Erró – distinguish their oeuvre from mean tendencies of Pop Art. Jim Dine even formulated in 1966, in a very clear way: "I am not a Pop artist;" strangely his statement was not really listened at that time.

Jim Dine was completely aware of his distance to "hard core pop art," as it was understood in the 1960s. Instead of apologetic or even euphoric identification with the present moment, with the material civilization of the new urban society, the oeuvres of Jim Dine and Erró seem to have a tendency towards an excessive imagery, towards unconscious fantasy, towards personal history and strong dramatic language. These all didn't belong to the aesthetics of mean stream New Realism, in contrary. But their engagement in the narrative is considered today, for our today's sensibility and thematic orientation as specifically authentic and significant.

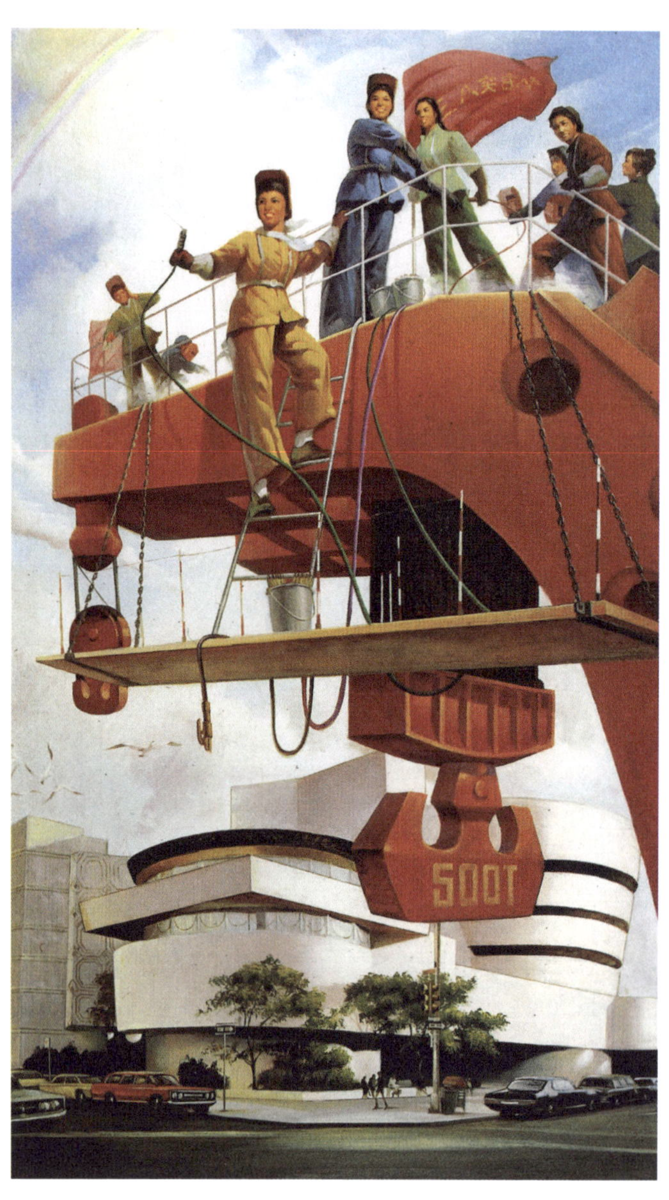

Erró
500 Tons, 1974
Oil on canvas, 180 x 100 cm
Courtesy of the artist

ERRÓ – AN ANTI-EPOS

The Irresistible Power of the Image or the End of Innocence

When Erró maintains in his essay, entitled *Se non è vero, è ben trovato,* that the art of painting is "a laboratory of the possible: a place where you can experiment, where you can do old things with new things,"[1] then he refers to an essential creative potential of the art of painting, i.e. the possibility to create *new realities,* which are located between empirical facts and imaginary fiction. When making a painting, one is capable of presenting a credible form of fiction. A painter will succeed in lending credibility and persuasive force to utopias – no matter how radical, how fantastic, how provocative and shocking they are. Through painting one creates pictures that manifest themselves as portrayals of an unknown reality. These are pictures that are not products of the creative processes involved when making paintings, but portrayals of realities that exist beyond the art of painting. The resulting pictures are not derived from fictitious and imaginary processes involved when making paintings, but from perceptions and reproductions of different realities.

In the "laboratory of the possible" pictures that are generated are perceived as new realities. Onlookers develop their own position vis-à-vis these realities, they regard them as real contexts of facts, points of reference, as well as perspectives that leave an impact on their orientation and judgments.

When making a painting, one has the potential power to put utopias and fictions into concrete terms, turning them into true realities, while at the same time demonstrating their aesthetic autonomy, their artificiality *par excellence.* This *artificiality* is provocative and confusing.

The more artificial the impression of a picture, the more credible it may be – which may sound paradoxical. After all, viewers will first look at the picture only as a picture, only as an artificial portrait of reality and will therefore strongly believe in this reality. The artificial nature of a picture does not question the truth of the really shown. On the contrary, it is exactly this aesthetic artificiality that gives legitimacy to the picture, as being a trustworthy messenger, an envoy, a mediator or a performer. The pictures of a possible reality that are created *in the course of painting* replace the pictures of an empirical reality. It is the power of a picture that turns the fiction into real existence, giving it credibility and an established status.

Erró's work suggests with powerful sensuality that the picture, the pictorial reality, the fictive-imaginary visual phenomenon may be stronger than the antique, confidential, banal, seemingly evident reality of the everyday life: it may become a new reality. And it is this new reality that influences the mental, ideological, cultural modes of thinking and produces, in turn, new realities, which contain the references of the simulacrum.

At this juncture, Erró grasps almost essential feature of the political significance of pictures in the western culture of late capitalism: namely the overpowering dominance of the simulacrum in our cultural, political awareness and our socio- cultural practices. In their essay *Modernity and Modernism Reconsidered,* Charles Harrison and Paul Wood state that the strategy of the "political economy of the sign" by Jean Baudrillad, which shifted the focus of questions regarding work and the production of goods to questions concerning the generation of messages and the production of systems of signs in the media, which is a typically western position, in contrast to the traditional Marxist viewpoint. In this connection, the point at stake was the change in cultural awareness in the highly developed Western and in the Far-Eastern industrial societies. "Baudrilllard was eventually to claim that reality itself had disappeared, lost behind the screen of signs. This is the condition from which the term 'hyperreality' become current in the later 1980s: a sense of living not in a world of work, production and real things, but a world of representations, of consumptions, of media images, of shifting surfaces and styles, a world in which the real has dissolved into a simulacrum. Clearly such a description is best going to fit, in fact to be derived from, an experience of the most extreme, all-encompassing examples of contemporary capitalism as it exists in parts of America and Japan. As its critics have pointed out, such a view is guilty of universalizing the experience of relatively few, relatively wealthy citizens of the world. It is nonetheless an experience, which rubs off on very many more – precisely through the operation of the mass technologies of the spectacle. One of its effects is to blur the edges of fantasy and reality."[2]

Erró is almost obsessed when working on manipulating the simulacrum; his basic material is mainly the visual *references* to different ideologies, political utopias, day-to-day political events and the popular forms of their visual presentation, ranging from posters and agitation brochures to pictures taken from comics and volumes of reproductions. What is most interesting about it is that Erró does not only create the picture of the simulacrum, but that, as a matter of principle, his basic material is the *ready-made picture* of the simulacrum. None of the components, none of the elements of his pictures are originals – in the sense of an individual, visual creation, of a personalized design – but existing pictures, bits of *ready-made pictures*, the function of which is to create a simulacrum.

In almost no other of Erró´s works but the *Chinese Pictures* we find a clearer and more obvious expression of the typical Erró method of creating subversive double layers, which first unveil, disarm and neutralize the world of pictures encountered in visual mass productions but the still cause one to feel the frightening power of fiction, the real danger of imaginary constructions, hallucinatory fantasies, visions, ideologies, religions. Erró presents the existing *ready-made pictures* that he finds in everyday life, in the world of consumerism, advertising, in art history (alive in reproductions), or political propaganda as insignificant visual material. In this connection, the surface carrying the visual information remains completely neutral, yet it suggests that everything could also be true, real and an actual fact.

His statement that "painting is a laboratory of the possible" tells us that everything which appears in a picture may become a reality one day, since there is something deeper and factual, something that is possible in perspective, behind the seemingly empty *ready-made pictures*, behind the existing banal sites of images. He does not primarily mean the power of pictures, since he treats

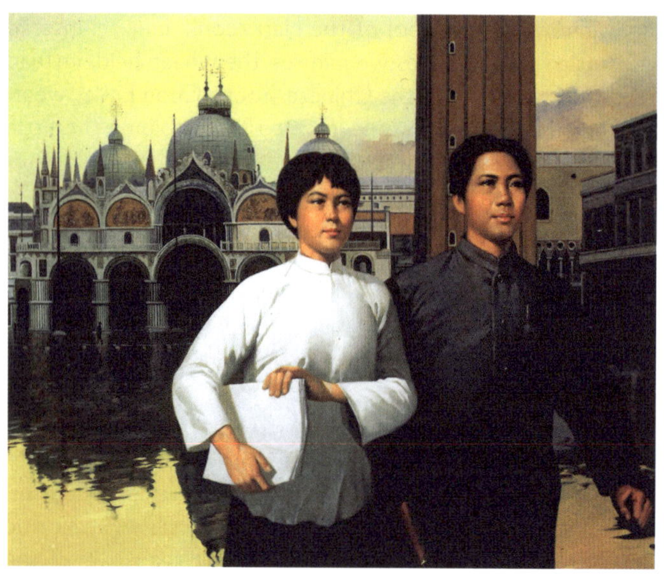

Erró
Mao and His Wife in Venice, 1976
Oil on canvas, 80 x 100 cm
Courtesy of the artist

the material of his pictures with complete aloofness, with complete neutrality; rather, he means something much more frightening, i.e. the real possibility of letting fiction become reality.

In his picture *Mao in Paris,* dating back to 1972, he presents – in the reality of a picture – a political paradigm of the Maoist theory regarding the expansion of the revolution to the western industrialized countries of the late capitalist era and the radical re-structuring of capitalist society, marked by exploitation and class hierarchies: in bright sunshine, Mao walks along a wheat field (with a smile and at a steady pace, full of optimism and aware of his goal), and he leads a group of young Chinese farmers and soldiers, fighters for the communist revolution at the war front of work, ideology, as well as anti-imperialist wars, followers of the dictatorial leader of the Cultural Revolution. However, they are not marching down any random place in China, but along a symbolic location: a transformed Place de L'Etoile in Paris – in front of the Arc de Triomphe, the symbol of the Napoleonic Empire. Instead of Parisian cobblestones we can see the wheat field; instead of the cars we can see the Chinese. Young Chou En-lai, wearing a military uniform, walks next to Mao, holding the little red book in his hand, and this gesture says it all: as long as the people faithfully follow Mao, as long as they believe in the world revolution, they will gain victory over the western world, they will be able to fight imperialism and class societies, then people will live in equality and prosperity. And the proud cities of the big imperialist powers will turn into wheat fields, the power of imperialism will collapse.

The 60 *Chinese Pictures*, which were created between 1972 and 1975, do not only criticize the myth of the Maoist Cultural Revolution, which was perceived as a radical alternative to western imperialism (but also to the model of the post-Stalinist, bureaucratic centralism of the Soviet Union), but primarily the power of the picture-like information that we find always and everywhere, of the sites used by propaganda, of the icons produced in diverse shapes and gigantic quantities that communicate ideologies in narrative forms, the heroes of the Cultural Revolution, permanently accompanying the masses in their everyday life and reminding people of the goals and perspectives of the world revolution at all times. This simulacrum actually serves as reality, where ideology and utopia become apparent in immediate connection with everyday life. The political leaders are always among the people; the masses shape history, under the leadership of their great guides.

The *Chinese Pictures* are assembled exclusively from existing and found pictorial material, such as the *ready-made pictures* from the world of comics, the paintings of official state art, scenes from Chinese and western films, posters and brochures and the didactic picture sites of political propaganda material. In a most ingenious manner Erró blends the fixed components of pathetic, apologetic Chinese agitation and propaganda with the hostile, simplifying, terrifying clichés of anti-western propaganda, with both sides using the methods of mystification and brainwashing.

Fiction is put into triumphal concrete visual terms, the hedonistic and sumptuous presentation of visions of the future become today's everyday reality, the world is put into simplified terms and society is divided into good and evil, the future is anticipated at the *present moment* – this makes the utopias, especially the ideological utopias, credible and imaginable: By repeating the narrative elements and idolizing fiction, the didactic, metaphorical stories become real *history*.

Erró employs exactly this double visual strategy: he demonstrates the perpetual potential of the picture, as an instrument that creates reality. With this instrument he unveils the manipulation strategies that abuse the visual, the fictitious for their own interests and without any scruples. Although the face of a seemingly "real" hero of the Cultural Revolution looks down on us from the monumental Mao pictures, we should not be deceived. Whatever appears to be an image of reality in these pictures is only the imitation of a feigned world, produced by ideology, where the political wishes and dreams are presented as a tangible reality of the present times. We are only confronted with a copy of a utopian fiction, which takes on concrete shape in the colorful, adventurous and gigantic simulacrum, designed with heroism and dynamism to entrap us, to force us to believe in them and, ultimately, to destroy our minds.

Putting Mao in well-known places all over the world reflects the messianic and utopian epoch of the 1960s and early 1970s. Erró talks about this quite often: "it was in the seventies. Before I became fascinated by the red pictures in Russia, it was the Chinese ideology that caught my eye, but it was political propaganda, of course. I found these images of great beauty and – above all – of great cheerfulness. The *Chinese Pictures* were much more interesting, technically speaking, than the Russian ones. The underlying principle of the work was to let Mao go everywhere, while, in fact, he traveled very little... I told myself it would be great to let him travel. To travel around the globe, without there being any bloodshed or aggression. And last year, at the exhibition at the Centre Georges Pompidou, I saw films showing the Beijing Ballet and I became aware that they got much inspiration from these illustrations. That was the origin of a large series of 140 or 150 pictures on the subject of that journey."[3]

What is so intriguing about this is that Erró utilizes the omnipotent, seductive, and aesthetic efficiency of irresistible, fictitious, and imaginative pictures to a maximum extent, as well as quite obsessively and hedonistically. His intention is to present, as authentically as possible, an ideologically imbued and fictitious travel report, the historically determined utopian credibility of an epoch serving as the basis of this aesthetic credibility. The ideological and utopian ideals were narrated in pictures as if they were real goals that could be achieved quite effortlessly. The simulacrum building on this belief created an aesthetically designed fictitiousness whose artistic efficacy elicited authenticity and credibility. Erró applies these very methods and models of aesthetic credibility and confronts models of simulacrum with each other to challenge the character of this fictitiousness.

The cheerfulness, the bucolic idyll prevailing in the sunlit fields, the smiling children and women, the workers proudly carrying the little red Mao book, and the soldiers following their leader with shining eyes are concrete proof that the dream of a perfect and ideal society can indeed come true; at the same time, they constitute a propaganda tool to persuade the population. The images of a just and joyful future world embody politically determined ideals. Thanks to the power exuded by the naïve, seductive, enjoyable, multicolored, cheerful, fictitious, and pictorial simulacrum, the ideal society of the future can be presented as an actually existing reality, as a fait accompli of sorts. This supplies emotional ammunition and facilitates ideological reasoning when it comes to making these ideals come true. In this sense, Mao's fictitious journey depicted in Erró's works reflects the naïve, voluntaristic, ideological, and strategic desire to conquer the world by means of the Maoist cultural revolution, the missionary zeal and conviction that people all over the world must be freed, as well as a critical articulation of the simulacrum that substitutes a fictitiousness legitimized and rendered authentic by the power of imagery for an existing reality. This replacement of real situations by a simplified and *efficient fictitiousness* forms the basis of Erró's subversive approach; the omnipotent pictorial element reinforces the hedonistic and fatalistic feeling that "everything is possible." The visual simulacrum is acutely real and impacts directly on influencing mechanisms and decisions.

Viewed from this angle, Erró's works appear quite critical, subversive, and political even though he refuses to accept any didactic or ideological function of art. However, there are clear indications of his commitment to subversive irony, and to disclosing mechanisms of manipulation. Says Roberto Ohrt: "His system of contrasts that unveils the tacit agreement concluded between the symbol of human or natural beauty and its conversion to a standardized mass product used in an industrialized world of labor was soon transferred to the central contrast of time, and to the contrast between East and West or between freedom and dictatorship. Typical fragments taken from the East's propaganda theater of bureaucratic power structures are compared with their opposite numbers in the Western world. Ideological symbols – mother and child, teacher and student, man with flag, leader and his people, hermit and revolutionary, sanctity – were rarely invented where propaganda claims would like to make us believe. Since the early 1960s, when international tensions culminated, Erró had the signs of irreconcilable antagonism migrate between their worlds and toyed with switching identities imposed on either side of the Iron Curtain."[4] This "identity switch" is a very irritating, bewildering, and thought-provoking exercise that specifies the deliberately seductive quasi-hedonism of the artist's exuberant picturesque imagery of *fictitiousness* in the context of the simulacrum. The omnipotent and aesthetic efficacy of the fictitious picture creates a confusing situation, and it no longer seems possible to pinpoint political or moral identities. Courtesy of subversive irony, the "identity switch" is depicted in an entirely coherent pictorial world, almost like a natural reality. It goes virtually unnoticed, and because of its unobtrusive nature it has disastrous consequences. Erró's artistic involvement is thus expressed indirectly. The subversive, exemplary narration which harbors harsh, strident, and differentiated criticism of cynical influencing mechanisms and of simplifying, banal, pseudo-moral value systems functions on the basis of this very masking exercise: behind the lush, picturesque, seemingly immaculate, and coherent imagery lurks the unavoidable, indissoluble antagonism between simulacrum and

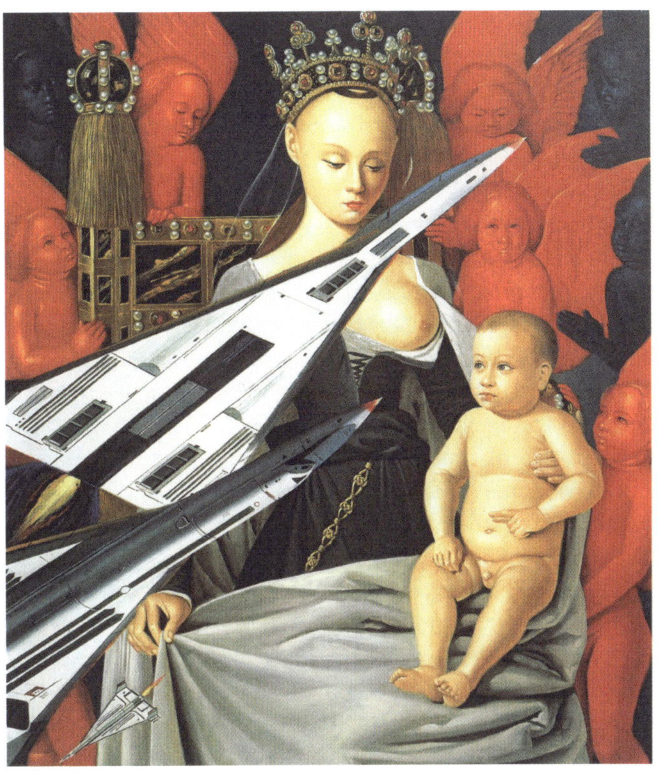

Erró
Decollage, 1974
Oil on canvas, 100 x 81 cm
Courtesy of the artist

human realities. The ominously interchangeable nature of seemingly diverging values discloses unbearable mechanisms of obfuscation and unpardonable lies.

From the outset, Erró has provoked us with the irresistible energy and power of his pictures and their images. The surfaces of his paintings teem with pictorial figures, so that there is not even the slightest hint of empty space, no free, unexploited area, not a single place without a scene. This inexorable, gigantic, at the same time sensuous, exciting, taxing and confusing flood of images, this omnipotent, breathtaking, but somehow also repellent stream confronts the viewer with how our contemporary culture is saturated with images to the point of absurdity. The surfeit of the pictorial, the unavoidable presence of the image everywhere, intended or not, interesting or tedious, pleasant or repulsive, dominates Erró's fictional-imaginative world and confronts the viewer, almost obsessively, with the question of the image's credibility.

May we even enjoy these pictures? Dare we indulge in the uncritical, irresponsible, luxurious hedonism of image consumption, yield to the lust of seeing, the "devouring" of visual experiences? Is what we get to see really altogether and perfectly delightful, or should we not listen – even for just a minute – to what the voice of doubt whispers? May the viewer really take these pictures seriously at all, or should we develop a critical-skeptical distance to them? Should we protect ourselves from the onslaught of this visual stream, steeling ourselves so as to be able to combat the seductive, bewildering, bewitching, sensual, visual power of these images? Should we pretend – in this context for moral reasons – to be blind, close our eyes so as to be able to resist the seductive impact of the sensual, light, superficial, manipulated pictorial dimension? Should we refuse to perceive the – seemingly flippant, irresponsible – hedonistic? Should we contrive deception, lull ourselves, pretending, as it were, to be innocent, and simply negate the real, seductive power of the image? Or should we internalize the subversive, critical perceptual system fashioned by the artist and operated with the same radical irony, in other words follow the artist?

Erró bombards us with these questions in the same vein as he continuously calls into question our aesthetic perception and ethical judgment with his overdosed, forceful pictures. But he is no cynical, even if operates with extreme irony. His questions are indeed the key questions of our "simulacrum society." Just how far or how much dare we believe in images? Is our enjoyment of the image still legitimate? Is the production of images itself still legitimate?

Already in his first large-format works he deals with the problematic of the overcrowded picture space as a metaphor of satiety. His fictive picture spaces are full of similar, almost uniform motifs, such as machines, industrial products, groceries or animals.

We have far too much of everything, we are saturated, in the physical sense, crammed full with objects and figures, consumer goods and animals, household goods and grocery products, we are insufferably full and unpleasantly overfilled with things which are thrust upon us in enormous quantities and cram our civilized space, our cities and dwellings.

This saturation with objects and figures, which leaves absolutely no free space for anything else, which leaves no imaginary place for anything non-purposeful, for anything non-useful, for anything unplanned, unusual, unforeseen, is taken up by Erró in a metaphorical sense however, whereby it is precisely the soul-destroying, unbearable absence of free space, i.e. the space of possibilities, of fantasy, creativity, improvisation, thinking differently, and ultimately the space of freedom, which compels us to revolt. Everything is full, everything is planned and occupied, everything is utilized; there is no air, no space, no alternative. It is precisely this feeling of saturation that is conveyed here, and Erró follows this with unwavering consequence until the end.

The wearisome abundance of wealth, this leaden saturation with the objects of early consumer society does not create contentment, a sense of wellbeing, but the opposite, dissatisfaction, discomfort, disquiet, because the sense of losing empty space is stronger than the sense of agreeable satiety and comfort. By exaggerating satiety and overindulgence, Erró creates indirectly the sense of loss, creates a need for the missing free space, because the absence of free possibilities and the vacant place, which one could fill with ideas and proposals, initiatives and improvisations of one's own, has a more emphatic impact than a feeling of material satisfaction and sensuous satiety.

This latent, veiled moral message, which localizes his aesthetic position as being within the broad context of 1968 revolt of ethical resistance against the hypocrisy of the early consumer society, determines his entire creative work, even if he later transfers this subversive, critical exaggeration of the feeling of satiety with things to the images of things, i.e. to the simulacrum. Through this a more complex, critical-analytical system arises, whereby focus is placed on the image, or respectively the gigantic image production, and no longer the real objects, no longer the physical accumulation of things. The countless colorful, partly highly interesting or striking, and yet simultaneously banal, well-known images create the world of the simulacrum, a world in which the consumer completely loses his/her critical relationship to real things and is now fully at the mercy of the fictional, imaginary, seductive, simulating images. These images present wishful thinking, fictive projections, models and clichés, which replace immediate realities. Becoming saturated by the images of the boundless, gigantic world of the simulacrum allows just as little free space for immediate, unplanned, unforeseen activities as the accumulation of consumer items and products, but simulates a certain perverted, risk-free fantasy, which through this manipulated pseudo-freedom belittles reality.

What emerges is a chaotic, interesting, colorful, picturesque, in part seductive picture in which everything is possible, in which the fictional and wishful thinking mingles with realities, whereby there are no longer any rationally comprehensible contexts, no causalities, no consequences, no logical sequence; instead we have a psychedelic, dizzying, relativizing synchronicity of all possible attitudes, of all possible references, and of cultural, ideological, religious legitimations, a juxtaposition of the most varied mindset systems and mental organizational forms. This incessant, hyper-intensive, mental vortex of the simulacrum fills the works of Erró with the frightening power of the image, where he confronts the viewer brutally, painfully and uncompromisingly with the consequences of the loss of innocence when looking at pictures.

There is no longer any innocence in our perception, when we look at and appreciate art! We can no longer simply enjoy the picture; the painter can no longer simply paint a picture. It makes no difference what he/she paints, from he/she takes the visual raw material, it is already manipulated, used, simulated. Even qualities like the decorative, the interesting and the picturesque are suspect: they canalize the attention of the naïve, innocence viewer and bewitch him/her with, mawkish or awful, interesting pictures, which draw in the really awful pictures into this seductive connection, into this dangerous alchemy and so relativize their believability. Erró sees this mechanism clearly and discloses it through his subversive strategy of pseudo-attractiveness. He goes much further down this path when he focuses so radically, so brutally on the loss of innocence in our perception. He leaves the viewer alone, bewildered and overwhelmed by the stream of images, and he exaggerates the provocative impact of hedonistic graphic pictorial representation. But it is precisely through this limitless and absurd exaggeration of pictorial representation that the mechanism of seduction and the boundless relativizing of realities are unveiled.

Erró is an extremely courageous artist, who even puts his own artistic credibility on the line so as to place his radical irony in the service of a subversive critique of the image. He lets his own methods and weapons be used in the playful world of the simulacrum to such an extent that at some point they generate the contrary impact: they reveal themselves to be pseudo-radical and enable us to understand that in their exaggeration the shameless banality of pictorial manipulation is ridiculous, primitive, empty. What is interesting here is that Erró can nevertheless show up the dangerous, cynically effective, seductive deceptive potentiality of this mechanism as a real threat, although his pictures continue to seemingly function perfectly as hedonistic-sensual commodities.

Erró is inexhaustible in his work; he is just as unflagging as his pictures. The irresistible impact of the pictorial is based on the radicalness of the subversive irony, which leaves us no chance whatsoever for making something beautiful, nor for recovery, which leaves no fabrication and manipulation undetected, whereby he repeatedly captures the shameless – and simultaneously banal, simple – manipulation strategies of pictorial composition and enlightens the viewer in a constant and uncompromising commentary. His subversive commentaries are fresh and strong, potent and powerful, but at the same time do not remain untouched by a genuine, deeper, hidden tragic, for he considers his visual subversion not exclusively as didactic-moralistic explanatory work, whereby the combative optimism unavoidably always generates a certain weariness and benevolent banality, but rather as an engagement with the puzzle of the image, whereby he knows exactly that the enigmatic in the image is also present when the image itself is manipulated and exploited. The enigmatic resides in how the impact of the image is far broader and deeper, more complex and contradictory than some functional system which deploys the image one-sidedly and fatally functionalistic, although it keeps its ability to hint at something more, something unexpected, something unforeseen, which in no case is incorporated in a single functional system. Erró can thus speak of the end of innocence, deploy his radical irony and nevertheless – or perhaps precisely for this reason – always retains the believability of the image.

Irony and skepticism, subversive humor and hidden moralization, shape the colorful, almost baroque, unbelievably diverse visual world of the legendary artist of the "Narrative Figuration," Erró. His activity combines the turbulent, radical, eccentric, rebellious 1960s with the skeptical, wary, medium-oriented 1990s, and then with the hedonistic years of the new millennium, unfolding in the boundless, nontransparent simulacrum. His "grand narratives" with their epical opulence, with their demonic, uninhibited hedonism, but above all with his critical relativizing of the image's believability, represents the grotesque panorama of the 20th century in its entirety, in a kind of provocative anti-epos.

The name Erró is inseparably tied with the term Pop Art, and thus with the far-reaching, radical changes the artwork undergoes in the age of consumerism, impacting on how art is viewed and appreciated in all its facets, which took place at the end of the 1950s or the beginning of the 1960s on both sides of the Atlantic. In specialist literature this period is described with the rise of the so-called English Pop Art and City Art, or the American New Realism and the French-Italian Nouveau Réalisme and the Figuration Narrative. The phenomenon of the German Kapitalistischer Realismus also belongs to this aesthetic orientation, even when the German artists were far more emphatic in their direct political responses and statements, and so the associated activist practice, than their American, English and French contemporaries.

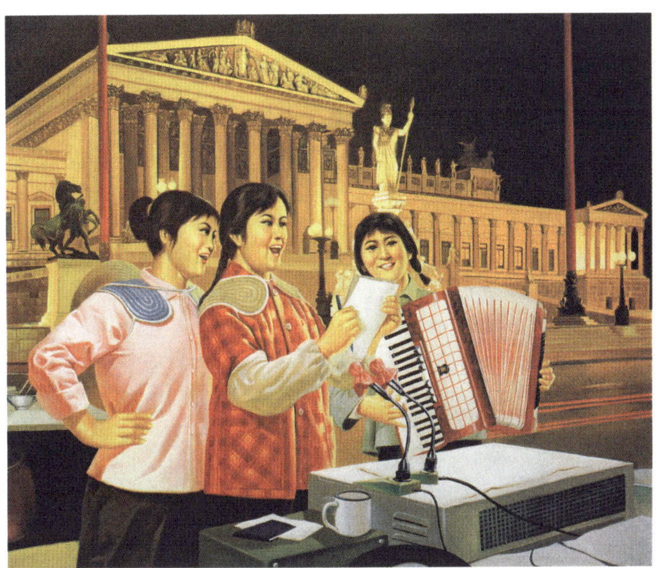

Erró
Vienne, 1979
Oil on canvas, 80 x 100 cm
Courtesy Mumok, Vienna

Although the Nouveaux Réalistes group from Nice is generally acknowledged as the main example of the new realistic and representational art characterized by irony and a critical stance on society, there was a large number of various groups in the French art scene at the beginning of the 1960s which took a very similar position, for instance the circle around Pierre Restany, but nevertheless were markedly different in terms of their political-ideological convictions. The Icelandic painter Erró, who moved to Oslo from Reykjavík as a twenty-year-old art student, and then later, in 1955, on to Florence and lived until 1958 in Italy, before moving to Paris, is one of those radical artists who organized a series of thematic group exhibitions over the course of the 1960s in Paris, which presented the aesthetic and political position of a new generation of artists committed to representational art critical of society.

All of these young artists opposed the lyrical abstraction of the École de Paris and the geometrical abstraction of the circle of artists affiliated to the gallery of Denise René, for they rejected abstract art as embodying an attitude that was too individual, esoteric, out of touch with social reality and so serving bourgeois interests, merely decorative and politically neutral. Refocusing their efforts on the figurative, for their part the radical painters sought to initiate a profound change in how we view and appreciate art, particularly in the area of defining the function of art: they wanted to create an art that was critical of society, analytical and actively involved in the processes of social reform, an art that through the shockwaves emanating from the ironic strategy of confronting arbitrary clichéd images with drastic reality was to rouse awareness of the power of the image.

The most important stations of this process of change were the path-breaking exhibition "This is Tomorrow" held in London's Whitechapel Art Gallery in 1956 and featuring the Pop Art collage by Richard Hamilton that was to quickly acquire legendary status, *Just What Is It that Makes Today's Homes so Different, so Appealing?*, a work that for the first time assembled direct social references from everyday life in early consumer society into ironic-provocative layers; this was followed by the *Manifeste des Nouveaux Réalistes* published by Pierre Restany on the 16th of April 1960, a manifesto in which he radically nullified the boundaries between art and life, between aesthetic value and banality, between artistic styles of form and the mass production of industrial society; and finally in 1962 there was the synoptic exhibition "The New Realists" held in New York's Sidney Janis Gallery, which presented the various parallel unfolding tendencies of New Realism in America and thus featured a wide range of young artists, like Rauschenberg, Jim Dine, Oldenburg, Wesselmann, Rosenquist, and Warhol, artists who were rebelling against the hegemony of Abstract Expressionism and the individual, aristocratic language of form and the pathetic Purism evident in *Informel*. What these manifestations share is the unequivocal and consequential rejection of abstract, esoteric, individual, gestural vocabularies of form which take an artwork to be the terrain for the radical self-expression of an artistic individual. Accompanying this, we may observe a growing interest in the sociologically identifiable and concrete objects and things of everyday life and consumer society.

Whereas those American artists who from the mid-1950s on were known as the New Realists, then later under the tag Pop Art, were less concerned with the political and social aspects of representing consumer goods and the mass media of modern industrial society, their European colleagues, foremost young artists in France, Italy and Germany, attempted to incorporate and show in their artistic activity the critical-ironic engagement with the – legitimated through the mass media – power structures of consumer society. Particularly in France there was an intensifying politicization of art from the beginning, one accompanied by an increasingly pronounced politicization of art and culture theory, which not only furnished aesthetic strategies – such as Pierre Restany for the Nouveaux Réalistes – but also formulated directly adaptable methodologies for radical revolutionary practice. In 1968 the art critic Michel Troche went so far as to demand that not only abstract art – in his view solely formalistic and merely serving to decorate bourgeois consumer society – needed to be done away with, but art as such. The theoretician Roland Barthes emphasized the demythologizing and enlightening function of art, whereby he focused on the aesthetic possibilities of a critical-figurative art in disempowering – legitimated by the power of the images produced by the consumer world – quasi-mythologies.

Besides the three aforementioned exhibitions bringing these artistic endeavors to light for the public, other important exhibitions were staged in France, which presented the varying tendencies of the new figurative, narrative art informed by politics, ideology, sociology. As early as 1961, a year after the founding of the Nouveau Réalisme, which quickly shot to fame, artists like Jacques Monory, Bernard Rancillac, Valerio Adami, Peter Klasen, Erró and Gérard Fromanger organized the exhibition "Nouvelle Figuration" in Paris. This group exhibition was restaged in 1962, this time with an even more intensive commitment to a political focus. The artists and theoretician Bernard Rancillac formulated the dual concerns of his aesthetic aspirations: they were not only seen as a countertrend to lyrical, informal abstraction, or the geometric, kinetic abstraction of the Paris gallery scene in the 1950s, but also aimed to engage social reality, whereby the artist was to not just represent visible reality but interpret and challenge it critically. In 1965 the large exhibition "Narrative Figuration" was held, featuring the work of 68 artists. Both exhibition titles express clearly the return of the figurative, i.e. an artistic commitment to render reality in images and to relate the subject matter like a story, albeit one that was to act as a biting commentary on social reality. Theoreticians of art like Alain Jouffroy and Michel Troche, artists like Bernard Rancillac and Gérard Fromanger were unanimous in emphasizing that this new figurativeness was not some reversion to the old realism – it was a committed exploration into and challenge to social and political reality.

As it became ever clearer, the basic theoretical conception of the new realism and figurativeness as social commentary and analysis of images in their role as the agent of power structures was soon adapted as the basic idea for period's most important exhibitions: the group exhibitions organized in 1964 and 1967 entitled "Everyday Mythologies." Artists such as Adami, Arroyo, Erró, Fromanger, Kermarrec, Klasen, Monory, Poli, Rancillac, Rebeyrolle, Recalcati, Veličković and Voss sought here to demonstrate that their figurative art was demythologizing and aimed at exposing the visual-pictorial manipulation of modern consumer society, which by virtue of the power of images and the sensuous-pictorial objectification of the "myths" of modern capitalist consumer-driven society only served to legitimate the direct interests of the powers-that-be – interests which included the diktat to consume as well as producing various forms of ideological repression and irrational obfuscation. The salient intellectual forerunner for this exhibition was Roland Barthes' legendary *Mythologies* (1957), a collection of texts in which the theoretician analyzed the power of images, namely the phenomenon of how in consumer society they managed to propagate concrete, banal, fleeting pseudo values as eternal and desirable.

The two large "Everyday Mythologies" exhibitions of 1964 and 1967 also graphically highlighted the different developments taken by American Pop Art and the Parisian Nouvelle Figuration or the Nouveau Réalisme in Nice. It was not just the politicization that was clearly given greater emphasis amongst the Parisian artists; the theoretical input was also more intense, exploring

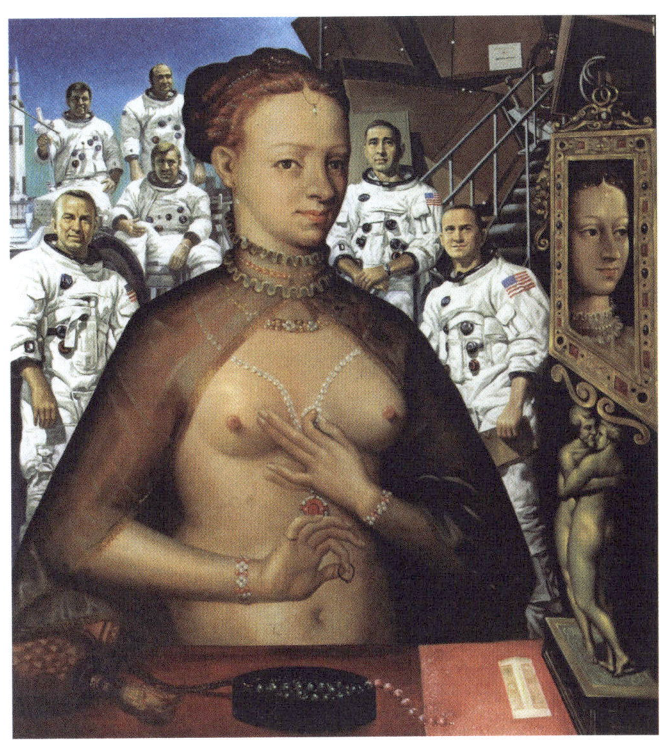

Erró
Diane et Apollo, 1975
Oil on canvas, 100 x 81 cm
Courtesy of the artist

the functions art plays in the process of dismantling hierarchical power structures, which in art are manifested in the manipulation of aesthetic values. One highpoint of this development was the major exhibition "Salon de la Jeune Peinture" in Paris in 1968, the year of the student revolt. The organizers Alain Jouffroy and Michel Tronche invited the artists to take part in a special exhibition, which under the title "Police and Culture" escalated the conflict between power and art, repression and freedom. Introduced by Jouffroy, the notion of "revolutionary individualism" served as the basis for this artistic manifestation where the artists not only formulated social-critical analyses of the repressive systems in modern capitalism, but also their own permanent struggle to gain the freedom bestowed by the imaginary, a pole around which the limitlessness of creative subversion should gravitate. This entailed an absolutizating of the irony with which the artists, as before them the Dadaists, sought to suspend and scupper everyday language as the communication system of the ruling powers and as the means for manipulating value representation in official society. They thus confronted banal everyday images taken from the consumer world – which the power of the mass media had turned into fixed objects of desire, although they in fact do not represent higher values – with the shocking images of brutal reality: poverty, terror, war.

It is not surprising that Erró, who following his return from Italy took part in all the collective exhibitions of the Nouvelle Figuration, painted his shocking, critical-realistic series *American intérieur* precisely in 1968, in which he confronts the naïve-mawkish, kitschy furnishings of the American lower middle-classes, featuring the new consumer goods of the 1960s, with figures of Vietnamese partisans or the Chinese People's Army taken from posters and television reports, newspapers and propaganda flyers. On the one hand, these paintings show the political discussions of the tumultuous years around 1968, the period when leftwing students and intellectuals interpreted the Chinese model as an alternative to European and American capitalism, when the war in Vietnam directed political attention to the so-called Third World, but also raised the question of the moral justification of Western intervention; on the other hand, they attempt to address the clichéd thinking and processes triggered by the psychological crisis that Western citizens believed to be caught in as they suddenly felt their stability and security, considered to be everlasting and unshakeable, to be in danger, turning the whole world outside the Western sphere into a threat. Erró's series illustrates his methodology: to confront visual clichés with other visual clichés. The various sections of the paintings are just as "pre-fabricated" as the consumer items fabricated by modern capitalism. Like the miscued perspective on the "enemy," one's own world is also viewed through clichés. Composed of advertising and department stores, of television and illustrated magazines, the sugary idyll manifests a superficial naivety, utterly blind towards reality, just like the image of the hostile, aggressive, threatening "other" world television reports and kitschy adventure films manipulatively fashioned from intentionally simplified, clichéd images.

The Iceland-born painter Erró, once going by the name Guðmundur Guðmundsson, worked in Florence with this friend Jean-Jacques Lebel between 1955 and 1958. As a restorer he was involved in work at the San Vitale in Ravenna. His profound interest in art history, which later comes to light so incisively in the series *Sex-Trémités* (1958-1969) and *Retour d'USA* (1962-1963), stems from these years spent in Italy. In Milan he became acquainted with the abstract painters Prampolini and Capogrossi, in New York the Nouveau Réalisme artist Arman and a few American artists involved in the Pop Art scene such as Jim Dine, Roy Lichtenstein, Robert Rauschenberg, Larry Rivers and John Chamberlain, in Paris the Swedish multimedia artist Öyvind Fahlström and the exhibition creator and later director of the Centre Pompidou, Pontus Hultén.

All of these acquaintanceships intensified his interest for a new, objective, impersonal, figurative art which integrates objects of everyday life and fragments of everyday situations – such as advertising, shop window displays, newspapers and illustrated magazines, comics – into an autonomous visual world without succumbing to an aesthetic prejudice. From the outset, Erró sought to absorb the motifs of the new technological world, above all machines and constructions, in his paintings. Coming face to face with American Pop Art and discussing with the new generation of artists in the United States and France urged him more and more to try out and elaborate a new form of figurative representation in painting. Like his Parisian friends Jacques Monory and Eduardo Arroyo, he developed a visual language which, with increasingly clarity, represented the visible world in a cool, impersonal, photo- or film-like manner, a visual language which, from the very beginning, revealed a complexity of pictorial references from banal everyday life, from modern, up-to-date, fashionable consumer world, from politics and contemporary events, but also from art history. Whereas Arroyo, Monory, Klasen and Rancillac operated extensively and consciously with photographs from dailies, film reports, television news and well-known images circulating in the mass media, Erró also fashioned his diverse, complex visual world with fragments and specifically identifiable details taken from art history.

From the mid-1960s, in particular after a longer stay in the United States, Erró increasingly worked with the "pre-fabricated" images of illustrated comics, whereby he often incorporated – like the American Roy Lichtenstein – the speech bubbles with a highlighted importance into the composition. The simple, often aggressive and primitive texts manifest a cliché system that is just as reduced and intentionally manipulated as the images, characterized by graphic simplification, strongly marked contour lines and reduced use of color. When Erró draws on pictorial fragments from art history which represent a different kind of ideological and aesthetic manipulation he is reflecting on the problematic of the constructed image and analyses its potential to convey values and moral judgments. The image is not only capable of reproducing visible reality one way or another, but also able of awakening certain intentions and clichés in its viewer, which through he/she is in turn supposed to consider reality. In this way the structure of meaning in an Erró painting gains a double character: on the one hand, the artist manifests the power of the image, which in the context of contemporary politics may be unequivocally interpreted as negative – and this dangerous potential is clearly revealed by looking at and understanding the picture; on the other hand, he alludes indirectly to modern consumer society and its mass media, and with this critique takes on an active role in the struggle to disclose systems of manipulation.

The presence of this combative, politically-motivated attitude is particularly strong in his collages, where he confronts certain ideological positions and clichés, illusions, prejudices with the brutal images of reality. Portraits of politicians, political logos and emblems of the various movements, typical motifs in circulation and well-known – symbolic – places, events hyped up in the mass media, documents often shown in newspaper and television reports: all these elements are assembled into a provocative and revealing visual kaleidoscope, with the viewer feeling aggravated by the sheer elementary force of the images. The technique of collage seems to be particularly suited for this fresh, immediate, provocative and aggressive juxtaposition between various reference points. The creative fantasy and the boundless associations enliven the narrative of these collages and make this technique an ideal experimental field for the larger painted compositions.

In Errós painting *Cobra et Provos* from 1967 we see portraits of figures from the Amsterdam youth protest movement, confronted by pictorial details typical of the painters of the Cobra Group, for example the face by Asger Jorn, or fragments by Corneille and Alechinsky. On another painting from the same year he brings together ironically painted apes with details taken from Matisse and Derain. In the series *The Aggression* from 1967-1968 he montages the well-known figure from Munch's famous painting *The Scream* with an American fighter jet from the Vietnam War. The primordial fear, which in the work by the symbolic-expressive painter Munch is expressed so unforgettably as a perpetual and unalterable state of human existence, is here at once relativized and brought up to date through the juxtaposition with the current war situation – a concrete shot from the Vietnam War: the cult painting of Early Expressionism loses its generally valid, universal, i.e. its aesthetic meaning, and is reinterpreted into a concrete, banal, real depiction of actual fear in the face of terror and death in a specific, real war situation. One could even say that the aesthetic aura is radically destroyed here so as to be able to capture the true reality of human angst in a concrete, physical situation of modern warfare. But here Erró is working on the metaphorical level as well: he has to sacrifice the image, he has to destroy the aesthetic autonomy of the work, and he has to break through the walls of the stronghold protecting aesthetic sublimation so as to lead the image and the painting back to reality.

In the following years this tendency becomes more and more incisive and crystallizes into the main line of Erró's art. From the mid-1970s, in particular since the series *Leger* from 1977, he has increasingly operated with quotes taken from art history and visual fragments from the history of Modernism. The 1974 series *Chinese Paintings*, in which he translates Chinese communist propaganda declaring that the revolution shall conquer the world and liberate the working-class from its capitalist yoke across the globe into visual metaphors, brings face to face in a brilliantly ingenious arrangement the various image topoi of Western and Eastern political propaganda, ranging from the media reports on the successful conquest of space through to the socialization of agriculture and culture. Erró analyses the images of propaganda with stinging criticism and bitter irony: all that is false and simplified is enlarged to the point of absurdity, revealing its hollowness and the perilous eradication of any complexity.

Erró's oeuvre of the last ten years is marked by the unfolding of a sovereign, irresistibly hedonistic visual language, one in which he articulates an almost encyclopedic overview of his early years and complements this with elements taken from comics, animation films, computer-generated drawings and screen manipulation. The visual formats are sometimes given gigantic dimensions; the well-known men and women figures of the ironically heroised superman clichés represent an apocalyptic atmosphere at the close of the millennium in post-modern industrial societies, whereby the true emotions are denigrated to ridiculous, kitschy, degenerate pseudo-feelings and the action, the true aesthetic dramatic, the fundamental argument spurning the conflict and the struggle to change the world deteriorates to a miserable Hollywood-like pseudo-actionism. This colorful, apparently attractive, apparently dynamic world is exposed by its very own visual clichés. The viewer feels to be forced into the dual role of voyeur and accomplice to a manipulation process no longer under his/her control. The demythologization determines how the work is viewed and appreciated, and its resonance is so far-reaching that following the study of these pictures, skepticism is the sole valid stance towards the powerful clichéd images and the efficiently functioning manipulation systems.

This skepticism – as "negative history," as "anti-epos" – fills the narrations of the encyclopedic visual world created by this great "fresco painter" of the 20th century. Erró shows us the world as being at once diabolic and grotesque, whereby the clichés and prejudices, the naïve glorification and horrific experiences render questionable and indeed dubious any unambiguous and clear orientation claimed by our value systems and worldviews. The unbearable weight of empty clichés reveals at the same time the superficiality of the pictorial when it is fashioned and shaped by the mass media, as well as the true dangers of manipulability, aggressiveness, repression and hopeless disorientation lurking behind these intentionally theatrical, seemingly rich, diverse and adventurous settings.

In this context it becomes clear that Erró – despite his provocative, contemporary *par excellence* and critical pictorial innovations, or paradoxically precisely through this revival of narrative painting – is one of the great Critical Realists of European culture, on a par with the great narrators like Balzac, Dostoevsky, Flaubert, Pirandello or Musil, all of whom brilliantly presented the horizon and mechanics of the "big stories" in ever-recurring "small events." Erró's power is the power of the sovereign image, the suggestiveness triggered by the irresistible, productive, unavoidable stream of images which turn our feelings and projections, intellectual deliberations and emotional experiences, our fears and hopes, disappointments and illusions into colorful, powerful pictures, whereby the picture – by virtue of the subversive irony – faces us as a potent mirror. His provocative, critical, analytical "anti-epos" operates with a strategy that radically relativizes ideals and values, while simultaneously maintaining a claim to capture and present totality, a claim that paradoxically allows his "anti-epos" to be understood as a continuation of the grand historical epopee.

(2003-2013)

1. Erró: "The Discontinued Story 'Se non è vero, è ben trovato,'" in: *Erró*, catalogue, Museum of Modern Art-Ludwig Foundation, Vienna 1996, p. 36.
2. Charles Harrison and Paul Wood: "Modernity and Modernism Reconsidered. Originality and Appropriation," in: Paul Wood, Francis Frascina, Jonathan Harris, Charles Harrison: *Modernism in Dispute. Art Since the Forties*, Yale University Press, New Haven and London 1994, p. 241.
3. Erró: "Mémoire effacée. Erró interviewed by Hans Ulrich Obrist," in: *ERRÓ*, catalogue, Galerie Hilger, Vienna 2005, p. 50.
4. Roberto Ohrt: "Alle Grenzen werden fallen. Deserteure aus dem Theater des Kalten Kriegs," in *Erró Fahlström Köpcke Lebel*, catalogue, PhoenixArt, Hamburg 2003, p. 89.

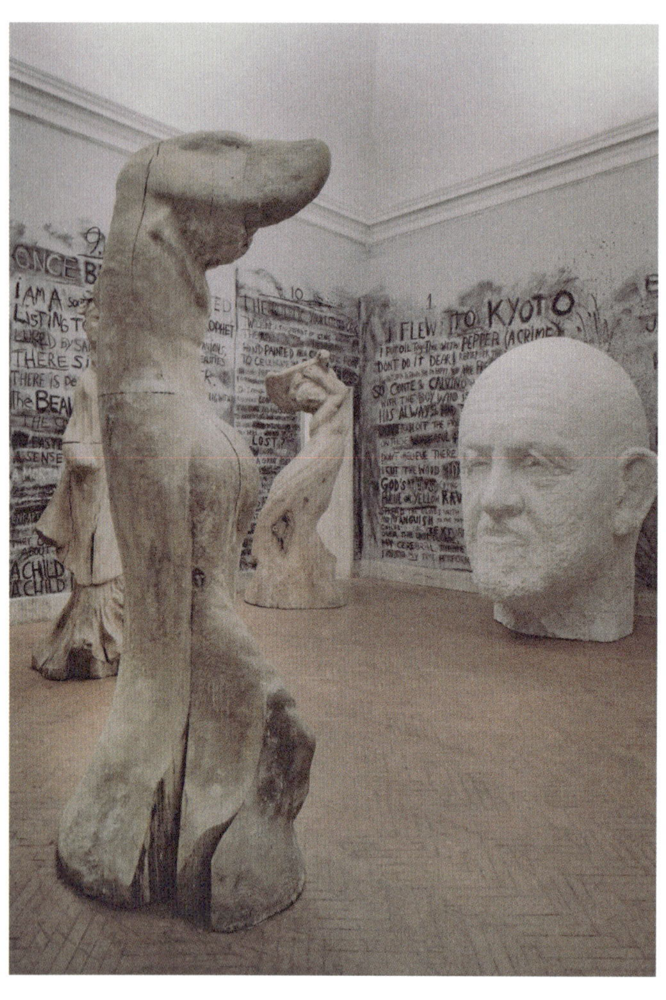

Jim Dine
The Flowering Sheets (Poet Singing), 2008-2016
Polystyrene, plaster, wood, charcoal
Courtesy of the artist and Richard Gray Gallery, Chicago-New York
Installation view of the exhibition "Jim Dine. House of Words. The Muse and Seven Black Paintings," Accademia Nazionale di San Luca, Rome, 2017-2018

JIM DINE – POETIC AUTHENTICITY

"I am Happy to be a Prisoner of my Ageless Emotions"

"I came away with the idea of a matrix of my head and ears that I could fill with some sort of painting, that was about paint, that applauded paint, while still keeping a personal vestige of self-portraiture. Everything I do is self-portraiture."
(Jim Dine in a conversation with Michael Rooks, 2017)

"The speedup in history-making has now reached the point where the interval of critical evaluation seems to have become superfluous. It is increasingly believed that all standards have gone down before the onslaught of the new and that the attempt to establish values in art may as well be abandoned. Brian O'Doherty reported that many people now think that it is more important for art to be avant-garde than for it to be good. Mr. O'Doherty himself went further: it had become, he claimed, more important for art to be advanced than for it to be art," Harold Rosenberg wrote in his critical essay *The New as Value*[1] with reference to an article by Brian O'Doherty published in "The New York Times" in July 1963. In his essay, Rosenberg analyzed one of the central topics of debate in the New York art scene at the time: the relationship between radical artistic innovations and artistic value, between what was "new" and what was "good." Is it "new" and/or "good" – or is it "new" and/or "art" – was the typical question of the late 1950s and early 1960s, when the young artists of the new Pop Art movement rebelled not only in a quasi-general way against established, intellectually recognized Abstract Expressionism, considered as almost synonymous with modern art and as the highest stage in the development of abstract art, but also against the moralism, intellectualism and existentialist pathos of abstract art, which to them seemed removed from real life, formalistic and academic.

Although the historical and formal connection between Abstract Expressionism, Action Painting and Combine Painting, as well as happenings and performances, is completely evident and undeniable in the historical genealogy of Pop Art, especially in the case of Robert Rauschenberg and Jasper Johns, a dividing line was strictly and inflexibly drawn, in keeping with the times, between

– on the one hand – euphoria for everyday life, the synthesis of life and art, optimism, hedonism, and the cult of the banal objects of everyday reality in the new consumer society, and – on the other hand – intellectual Abstract Expressionism, negating everyday reality and referring to universal values, dramatic, ethical and existentialistic.

The young artist Jim Dine, who had moved to New York just a few years before and had not only become well-known by the late 1950s and early 1960s, but had also come to be counted among the most significant and radical performers and artists, answered this fundamental, though somewhat naïve and reductive question with a commitment to quality, authenticity and even to artistic tradition that may have surprised many adherents and fans of the new Pop Culture: "There's too much emphasis on the new, I don't understand why everything has to be new – that is the most destructive kind of attitude. It's all new [...]. You can't have a successful picture without the old standards of beauty."[2] What Jim Dine meant by a "successful picture" will be discussed at a later point; here, what appears of central, fundamental significance – and absolutely essential to his later work – is his cautious, critical reserve vis-à-vis unbridled euphoria about "the new" as having absolute, indisputable value. His unique position in Pop Art; his odd, idiosyncratic solitude as an artist; the dark, dramatic and emotional world of his paintings; his obsessive examination of dreams, memories and certain constantly recurring themes such as self-portraits or tools; his interest in everything obscure and occult, enigmatic and fragmentary; his exploration of Jungian psychoanalysis – all these elements exhibit a poetic aura that is hyper-intense, open and marked by inner tensions. This dense, poetic narrative is fleshed out by a constant search for hidden and latent, yet crucial and fundamental determinations and fateful influences.

As a painter, performer, poet and printer, Jim Dine has never been unconditionally and exclusively interested only in "the new" in art. He was certainly never obsessed with "the new," unlike many of his fellow artists and many art critics of the time; he considered "the new" in art as something logical and necessary, springing from life as a normal manifestation of the new reality of everyday life, but saw it neither as the goal of artistic work, nor as the basis for the value of a work of art. His aim was not to create something fundamentally "new" – even if he was certainly always searching for new technical solutions, new techniques and materials – but to create powerful, emotional, touching and authentic paintings. He used new technologies and painting techniques, various inventions and compositional models to build his own personal, authentic visual universe, seeking to manifest and convey what he felt to be essential, singular and true, his entire dramatic worldview and his poetic emotionality.

Instead of unconditional euphoria for "the new;" instead of optimism and an affirming, hedonistic perception of the new, urban, technology-dominated everyday life; instead of the young consumer society's cult of objects; instead of worshipping anonymous mass culture and its mechanical production methods, Jim Dine's position as an artist manifested a poetic perspective that was complex, introverted and existential. Marked by a continuity of cultural history, replete with real, emotional and paradigmatic antagonisms, somewhat somber and rough, certainly not light and optimistic, profoundly subjective and sensitive, conveying the impermanence, sadness and fragility of life, it reflected elements of his personal micro-history and moments of his micro-social history, his biography and his origin, his earlier psychological problems, all his wanderings and elective affinities. Spiritual and emotional energies, fears and hopes, memories and imaginings, ideas from the depths of the past and experiences emerging from life operated in this coherent, poetic microcosm, linking the present with the past, with personal and collective memory.

"Despite its carnival aspects, its orgiastic color and giant scale, Pop Art's alternative to the emotional and technical impastoes of its immediate predecessor was clearly based on a tough, no-nonsense, no-preciosity, no-refinement standard appropriate to the 1960s. The choice of a 'teenage-culture' as subject matter contains an element of hostility towards contemporary values rather than complacency; it marks a new detachment from the accepted channels of art. Yet Pop is nowhere a nihilist trend. [...] the underlying mood everywhere seems one of determined optimism – optimism against odds, an optimism not always rec-

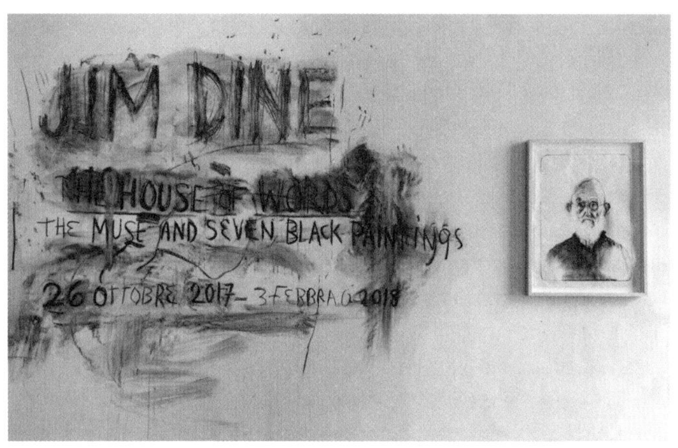

Entrance to Jim Dine's exhibition "House of Words. The Muse and Seven Black Paintings," Accademia Nazionale di San Luca, Rome, 2017-2018
Photo © Lóránd Hegyi

ognizable to those viewers who do not share it," claims Lucy R. Lippard.[3] This optimism also involved a fresh, bold, youthful, quasi "innocent" questioning of pathos-laden Abstract Expressionism that was marked by existentialism and spirituality, and a joyful apotheosis of contemporary, urban everyday life.

Partly disrespectful and partly banal, the young Pop Artists' ironic, critical and subversive anti-intellectualism was directed against the exaggerated, pathos-laden, absolute and almost obligatory adulation of the aesthetic and ethical values of transcendental abstract art, understood to be the true, authentic, incontrovertible and final, perfect manifestation of modern art. The cheerful, cheeky rebellion against the spirituality, pathos, purism, existentialism and moralism of post-war abstract art also came with liberating, youthful spontaneity and an anti-hierarchical, anti-conventional openness to the realities of everyday life, seeking – as Dada once had – to demolish the mythical and mythologized divide between life and art, the sacred and the profane, law and high culture, and ultimately to demolish the cultural hierarchy, though without aspiring to universalistic, fundamental and consistent revolution.[4] The integration of the social, political and ideological elements of the entire practice of art, and the expansionism and functional determination of the new art as an anarchical, subversive process of liberation, required a general vision of artistic work as a vocation to change society, though the earlier, pathos-laden, purist ideas of Abstract Expressionism were of course to be avoided. In this context, it should be noted that none of the movements and formations of so-called "Neo-Dada," "Fluxus," "Situationism," "Neo-realism," "Capitalist Realism" or "Figuration Narrative" involved any comprehensive, revolutionary theory, nor any consistent, political project for the fundamental remodeling of capitalist society as the ideological basis of their strategies. In fact, sometimes the contrary held true: they venerated subversive actionism, imaginative spontaneity, anti-conventional improvisation, anarchical questioning of all hierarchies and all projects, of politics really, per se. Even if there was often talk of revolution, no political or ideological strategy for revolution was elaborated, let alone any pragmatic, real politics planned for the new, alternative and open society to come after the revolution; instead, a spontaneous, cheerful, anti-hierarchical practice of self-liberation was proclaimed and, above all, experienced.

Pierre Restany, although he advocated erasing the division between art and life, also vested a special, even "magical" capacity in the work of art, thus maintaining its specific entity and autonomy. Contrary to the avant-garde of Russia's revolutionary years or in Germany, he never presaged a universal revolution, a total reorganization of society in political and structural terms, or a fundamental change of class structure, but rather spoke of a subversive shift in aesthetic values, a shift in perspectives on art and life, on artistic and non-artistic realities. Restany suggested a specific mission of art instead, speaking – especially in the case of Yves Klein – more of a mystical vitalization, a dynamizing of energies and connections between diverse spheres of the cosmic constellation. "Restany declared the Nouveau Réaliste appropriation of the readymade to be an affirmation of socially and aesthetically expanded notions of the work of art, which, instead of maintaining the division between art and the everyday, aimed to erase. [...] His insistence on the fact that Nouveau Réaliste objects were not anti-art and his ambition to demolish the art and everyday divide through the inclusion of the social

– albeit without eradication of the work of art as an aesthetic construct"[5] shows the significance of ideological interest in the various European discourses of Neo-realism.

In the context of the art of German "Capitalist Realism," the entire issue of politics and cultural criticism in contemporary artistic practice was focalized even more and often set at the center of the culture debate, even though the ironic, impertinent and subversive "destabilization" of the conventional values of bourgeois society and culture did not involve any radical, revolutionary strategy. The "Figuration Narrative" group of artists was also much more politically engaged than their American counterparts. Erró's Vietnam series represented the ideals of everyman citizens of consumer society in direct confrontation with images of the brutality of war and of the various dictatorships. This ideologically tinged questioning of social realities, of indifference and selfishness when faced with suffering, also expresses a sort of criticism of the media society's hypocrisy and the consumer society's voyeurism.

In this, precisely, lies the paradox of Pop Art, or the contradictory perception of Pop Art: on the one hand, it was interpreted as contemporary art par excellence, as the radical, expansionist – and ideologically based – expression of the zeitgeist of the 1960s, and thus as rebellion, as "Neo-Dada," as an anarchical and emancipatory act of liberation; on the other hand, it was rejected as a kind of betrayal of modern art, a betrayal of abstract art, of the "autonomous" and "pure" form seen as universal, self-referential and intelligible, of intellectualism and ethical maximalism.

The ambivalent, sometimes contradictory complexity of the ideological and political positions of various manifestations of Pop Art has been described by Rolf-Gunter Dienst: "Though, on the one hand, Pop Art recognizes and condones the contemporary situation and lays down its position markers in painting, it feels the need, on the other hand, to critically point out certain conditions of these times and bring about change."[6]

The optimism that Lucy R. Lippard refers to means an affirming, positive and joyous attitude towards the modern life conditions

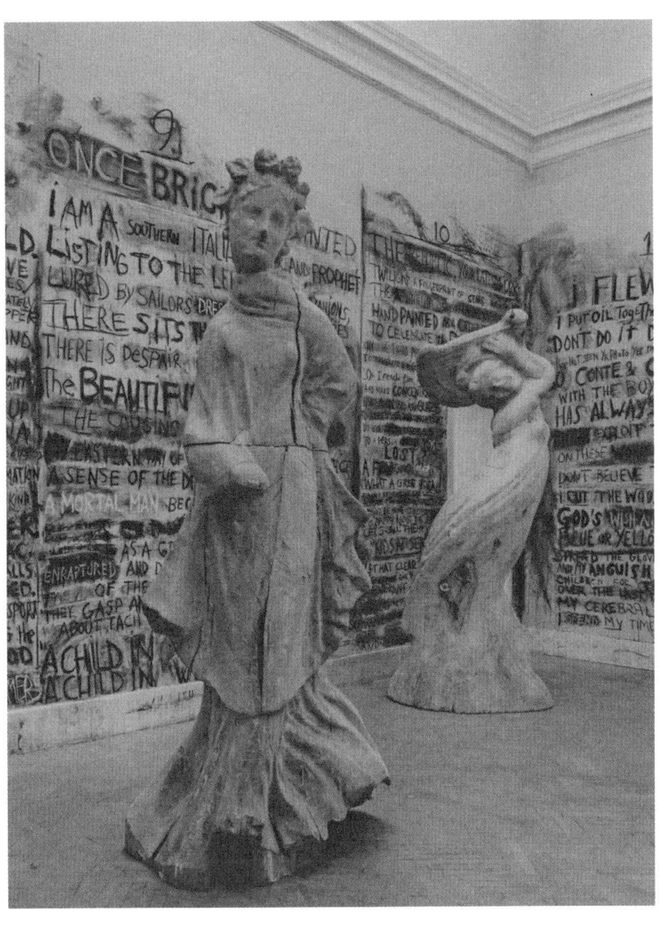

Jim Dine
The Flowering Sheets (Poet Singing), 2008-2016
Polystyrene, plaster, wood, charcoal
Courtesy of the artist and Richard Gray Gallery, Chicago-New York
Installation view of the exhibition "Jim Dine. House of Words. The Muse and Seven Black Paintings," Accademia Nazionale di San Luca, Rome, 2017-2018

of urban consumer society, and towards anonymous everyday modernity, built on mass production and technology, which also promoted a sort of anonymity, collectivism and conformity, replacing the individual, emotional self-representation of the artist-as-subject with the representation of the material realities of everyday life, or mass-reproduced multiple images of mass culture.

Affirming optimism, impersonal materiality and mechanical reproduction of multiple images of everyday life; the legitimization of a joyful perception of consumer objects; star worship and product worship; openness to "law culture;" the use of new, "non-aesthetic" or "unaesthetic" materials; collectivism and mass culture – all this created a new cultural climate, in which the fundamental, intellectual and aristocratic narratives of the post-war ethics and aesthetics discourse were critically judged and rejected. "As the 1960s were ending, traditional high culture seemed to be under siege by an even more pernicious threat: a counterculture that glorified drugs, unbridled hedonism, and license to 'do your own thing,'" Alice Goldfarb Marquis wrote about the zeitgeist of the 1960s.[7] She was analyzing the Metropolitan Museum's famous exhibition "New York Painting and Sculpture, 1940-1970," which marked the first time that a highly significant institution showed a comprehensive presentation of the contemporary trends of the time. The exhibition was curated by Henry Geldzahler, whose selection seemed completely arbitrary, problematic and extremely subjective to many art critics: "Critics of 'Henry's Show' also seized on Geldzahler's catalogue essay, in which he described his selections as 'a marriage of history and the pleasure principle.'"[8]

This joyful, indulgent, even hedonistic approach to art, in turn, espouses a fundamentally different idea of the function and meaning of artistic activity than the post-war era's Abstract Expressionism. Enjoyment, affirmation and even a euphoric view of contemporary, urban everyday life, as well as the actual, emphasized presence of material, banal objects and socioculturally identifiable, real places, were acknowledged as legitimate, as was – relatedly – a spontaneous, optimistic and affirming approach to everyday reality. Naturally, such openness presumed a critical position vis-à-vis the old moral and aesthetic conventions, the "old values." Openness and optimism, indulgence and hedonism, anti-hierarchical rebellion against high culture, curiosity for the new and approval of law culture went hand in hand in this subversive climate of change of the 1960s. As Lawrence Alloway put it with regard to the emergence of British Pop Art: "The area of contact was mass-produced urban culture: movies, advertising, science fiction, Pop music. We felt none of the dislike of commercial culture standard among

most intellectuals, but accepted it as a fact, discussed it in detail, and consumed it enthusiastically."[9]
Along the same lines, Rolf-Gunter Dienst also stressed the significant role of the enjoyment of modern, urban everyday life as an important source of inspiration for Pop Art: "Big city life, geared towards easily consumable pleasures, and the influences of the advertising and entertainment industries have led the young American artists to see their environment under aspects necessarily determined by the psychologically stimulating wares of mass culture and consumer goods."[10] Optimism, hedonism, anti-hierarchical and subversive openness; "easily consumable pleasures" and the "pleasure principle;" consumer society and modern everyday life; mass media, mechanical reproduction and new materials – all this formed the zeitgeist of the 1960s, which shaped the fundamental narratives of Pop Art and the various forms of Pop Culture. As Lawrence Alloway described it, "The term 'Pop Art' is credited to me, but I don't know precisely when it was first used. [...] I used the term, and also 'Pop Culture,' to refer to the products of the mass media, not to works of art that draw upon popular culture."[11]

A rather somber, introverted, ponderous and certainly not optimistic figure, Jim Dine, who never wavered in his deep loyalty to artistic tradition, seemed to position himself outside the zeitgeist – this daze of affirming, sometimes euphoric perception of contemporary, urban mass culture and hedonistic enjoyment of the novelties of the new era; this youthful, impudent rebellion against conventions, traditions and hierarchies; this subversive questioning of intellectual abstractions and the legitimacy of the sublime. Yet that perception does not seem to be completely accurate, especially in view of Jim Dine's active participation in New York's performance and exhibition scene of the 1960s and 1970s. His works were shown alongside the leading representatives of European Pop Art and Nouveau Réalisme at the Sidney Janis Gallery in October 1962 in the exhibition "The New Realists" of subsequent fame, and in many further exhibitions at the same gallery in the following years.

Despite his self-evident presence at such events and his great visibility in the early 1960s in all Pop Art exhibitions at the Mar-

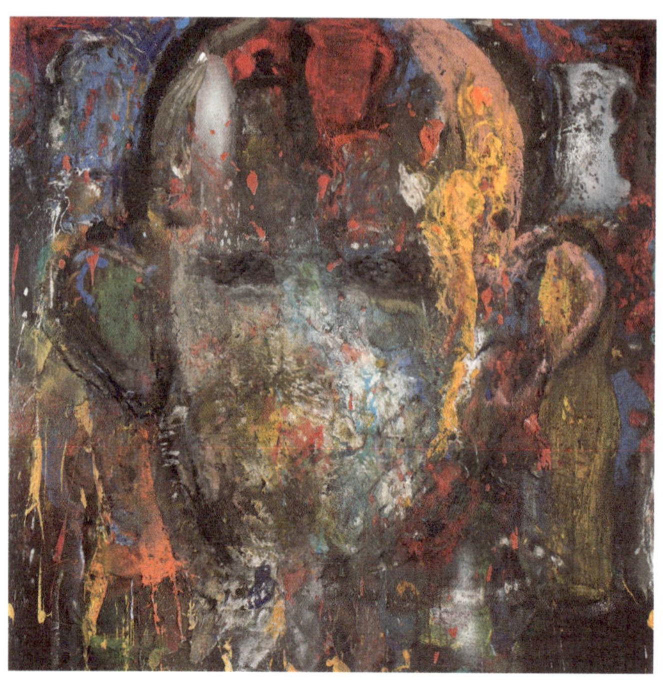

Jim Dine
The King in Blue Heaven, 2017
Acrylic and sand on Herringbone linen, 150.5 x 150.5 cm
Courtesy Galerie Templon, Paris and Bruxelles

tha Jackson Gallery and the Sidney Janis Gallery, Jim Dine's aesthetic place apart within Pop Art, and even partly in opposition to mainstream Pop Art, was recognized at a relatively early point. His strong connection to painterly tradition, causing him to put a new, radical, often dramatic questioning of narratives within the historically given framework at the center of his oeuvre, instead of a representation of modern, urban everyday life and its mechanical, technologized worldview, necessarily enhanced the subjectivity, emotionality and poetic connotations of his artistic expression. The enhanced, expressive intensity of his range of colors, and a frequently dramatic emphasis on the emotionality of shades of color – by no means just the typical colors seen in urban everyday life, sort of found in the street, used in advertising and industry, but rather colors that exhibit a sensuality reminiscent of German Expressionism – manifests Jim Dine's intimate connection to painterly tradition.

Similarly, traditional methods of handcrafting his works remained fundamentally important to Jim Dine, since they enabled him to convey his personal feelings and observations. Jim Dine remembers a conversation with Jasper Johns in 1963, in which his own path, his connection to old handcrafting techniques was clearly expressed: "I complained to Jasper Johns that my work was being treated badly because of its 'homemade' quality. He told me to get used to it as we are moving into an age of mechanical, anti-handcrafted art and there was no going back. He was right about what was to come and he was right that I wasn't going to go along with the prevailing winds."[12]

His doubts about "the new" as an absolute value, his deeply emotional approach to the material world – where he seeks human relationships, conflicts and stories, instead of merely demonstrating euphoria for "the new" – and his declared connection to old, non-mechanical methods of handcrafting his art set him apart, in a way: "In his 1963 and 1964 exhibitions at the Sidney Janis Gallery, Dine's preoccupation was clearly with paradox and parody, within the framework of older art. [...] Dine's parody does not hinge on the 'meaning' of the objects he uses, but on the way he uses them in a painting. He is not involved with subject or with new formal and pictorial devices, but with a complex and often redundant exposé of ways to paint."[13]

Even early on, many critics and art historians remarked on Jim Dine's aesthetic place apart in New York's Pop Art scene, his specific affinity to traditional art, and his work as a painter within a kind of traditional, compositional and thematic framework. In his book published only three years after the famously groundbreaking New York exhibition "The New Realists," the German author Rolf-Gunter Dienst expressed a truly essential observation about Jim Dine's specific aesthetic position among the movements of Pop Art: "With Dine, there is not so much critical engagement as the will to explore objects solely with regard to the extent to which they can be used as aesthetic objects for the painting. The object is never already a subject with artistic capacity, but only becomes such through its relationship to the painting [...]. Though Jim Dine is connected to the world of Pop images, the world of objects gains a value detached from the everyday in his works."[14] Thus, if one of the fundamental entities of Pop Art is to center works of art around the strong, demonstrative presence of the world of objects of modern, urban everyday realities dominated by technology and mass media, then Jim Dine's interpretation of the world of objects as a meaning internal to the painting and "detached from the everyday" is set outside the aesthetic intentions of Pop Art.

To legitimate "a value detached from the everyday," the artist needs a different basis of legitimacy – something that is not necessarily, directly or self-evidently reified in "the everyday," that is not automatically expected and legitimized by a culture or a sociocultural class, in a specific situation of cultural history or a specific moment; something intelligible and literary, then, something culturally mediated and historically fluid, something emotionally and psychologically amorphous. This is precisely what memory and remembrance can offer, the fictional and imaginary reification of virtual figures – mythical or anecdotal, ethnocultural, subcultural or micro-social – with intelligible, narrative substance replacing or supplementing so-called everyday reality, creating a blend of material and mental realities that functions as the source of the poetic narrative in the work of art.

Jim Dine's assertion that "you can't have a successful picture without the old standards of beauty" can be elucidated in this context. This is because the "old standards of beauty" are rooted in the metaphorical, evocative capacity of the painting, in which the concrete manifestation always points to something intelligible and metaphorical, to something that is absent and not apparent – to something mythological, communal, historical and anthropological. The triumph of the present makes absolute a focus on the contemporary object par excellence, on the objectivity and impersonal, mechanical materiality of modern everyday life, and it eliminates memory, the historical dimension and sensitivity to the past. Boris Lurie can be mentioned as the only exceptional figure in the New York art scene whose work as an artist focused obsessively and uncompromisingly on the genuine, personal ex-

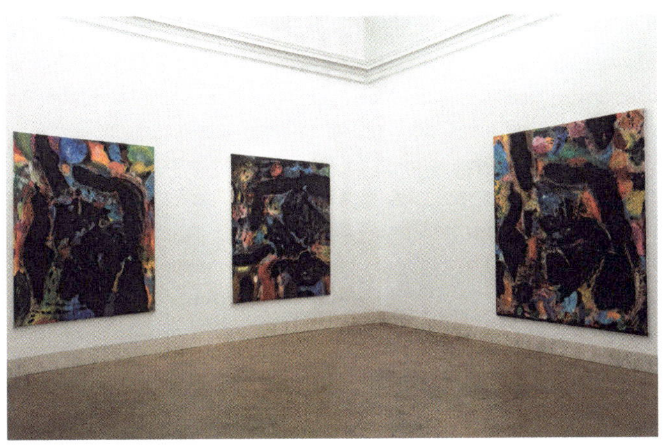

Installation view of the exhibition "Jim Dine. House of Words. The Muse and Seven Black Paintings," Accademia Nazionale di San Luca, Rome, 2017-2018

periences of his own life, and through this also on broader, more communal and ethical motifs. For Boris Lurie, the present served to reify the horrendous truth of the past; he used the realities of the present day to keep history in memory. Boris Lurie deliberately and unfailingly made memory absolute, with its sole, exclusive and necessary content – the annihilation of humans, the utter deprivation of liberty in the boundless helplessness of being totally enslaved and at the mercy of the Nazis' racism. In this sense, it could be said that the evocative, metaphorical narrative of Jim Dine's paintings and Boris Lurie's obsessive revisiting of history exhibit certain similar elements in the sense of extending the visual narrative to memory and shared experiences, though the fundamental, aesthetic differences between the two artists should also be emphasized.

In Jim Dine's poetic vision, the subjective, poetic and evocative involvement of the object in the complex, metaphorical narrative of the painting is given a central role. When Rolf-Gunter Dienst speaks of "a value detached from the everyday," he remarks precisely on the poetic, evocative capacity of Jim Dine's paintings – on the metaphorical expansion of the visual narrative, as the concrete, painted manifestation of objects of the present is integrated into an emotional and intellectual context that is uncontrolled, fluid and intelligible. Through this poetic, psychological, literary and anthropological complexity, expressed by means of rich references to cultural history and allusions to the history of art, the materiality of the present is interpreted not simply as given, objective, quasi "unproblematic" everyday reality, but rather as an extremely complex and multilayered, socioculturally determined context in anthropological, psychological, emotional, communal and linguistic terms, a context of the "history of humanity" in which history is both personal and universal.

In Jim Dine's art, the unfolding of such complex, poetic narratives can be observed from the very beginning of his oeuvre. It makes his works particularly authentic, as the various autobiographical and ethnocultural elements, references to cultural history, memories and imaginative connotations are all inextricably linked to his own life, his personal history and his cultural origin, and form a solid, compact and credible basis of legitimacy. Jim Dine writes about this in a beautiful comment: "At three years old, I remember sitting on the steps outside my grandfather's garage and taking pieces of pipe, of galvanized pipes, and rolling them down the stairs, just letting them go, like a Slinky toy, but it was pipe. I would just play with these objects of desire, like a hammer or I'd grab a screwdriver, and pretend to be an adult. I thought they were so beautiful. It was a non-verbal meeting."[15] Such a "nonverbal meeting" involves emotional, imaginative and connotative meanings – unconscious layers of meaning that have always had extremely great and fundamental significance in Jim Dine's overall narrative. Through this evocative capacity, a subtle, touching and poetically suggestive aura forms around the painted objects, expressing the actual meaning of the painting.

Jim Dine has actually never left the historically formed context of painting; rather, he has expanded, enriched, questioned and renewed this context, without connecting this renewal – inherent in painting – to euphoria for "the new" in spheres of life outside painting, to modern technology and mass media. He has often said that "you can't have a successful picture without the old standards of beauty."[16] Alice Goldfarb Marquis mentioned that Lawrence Alloway, too, had emphasized Jim Dine's unique position in an article published in 1962, at the very beginning of the emergence of Pop Art in New York: "Alloway had built a scholarly context around the artist, writing that he was not a Surrealist, as 'he does not distort the objects or place them in absurd contexts.' Rather, Dine 'brought the everyday object to a state of isolated glory.'"[17] This painterly interpretation of the objects was detached from the new, modern everyday realities, and sought to give the object its own value in the context of the reality of the painting, with even a latent, hidden and romantic approach to life, to personal events, appearing to be present.

This hidden emotionality, this romantic quest for deeper meaning – seeking not to grasp the novelties of the consumer world's new era, though they might be seductive and bewitching, but rather the inner life, memories and wishes, pains and hopes – is often expressed by self-destructive gestures, by ironic or parodistic self-interrogation, and by self-tormenting revelations. Self-irony appears to be a constant and fundamental entity of Jim Dine's poetic world. The playful, often bitter and complex scenography of self-irony set at the center of the structure of meaning, especially in his later years, and directly manifested, of course, in his numerous self-portraits and "alter ego figures" (Pinocchio, ape-people etc.), is latently and profoundly linked to the Eastern European Jewish cultural tradition, to its puns, its love of dark humor and jokes, to Jewish theater and modern literature. This somber, obscure, yet also ironic and dramatic entity of Jim Dine's art is perhaps given an even greater presence in his performances and writings than in his paintings and sculptures, or rather explains his tendency to seek verbal and dramaturgic forms of expression. His essential interest in theater, drama and poetry has shaped his entire work as an artist from the very beginning and has become apparent in various creative periods, such as the London years or his first years in New York, when he became one of the central figures of that era's performance scene, but also in present times, in recent years, when he has devoted considerable time to his poetry, and to his new, thematic and rather expressive series of paintings, marked by an evocative, literary narrative.

In this context, it should be stated that Jim Dine has always accorded particular importance and fundamental interest – in his paintings just as in his poetry, in his performances just as in music

– to a kind of constant self-interrogation, an obsessive search for his self and his essence, for his body and his place in time and in the world. His self-portraits are an embodiment par excellence of this narrative, with self-tormenting, dramatic and dark elements closely mingling with self-ironic and parodistic elements. This connects the different media and genres of his entire oeuvre, but also – in a more profound and general sense – the entirety of his narrative, and also creates a poetic coherence and compactness, with figurative paintings conveying the same narrative as object assemblages.

This dense, complex narrative, shaped by psychological problems, personal, micro-social and historical memories, concrete experiences and intelligible moments, stems from his deep, irreversible and essential rootedness in his own history, his family's history, his cultural, intellectual and historical origins, from the deepest layers of memory, where the personal, private self blends with the communal, multiple self. "My poem is about making a portrait, running after yourself. The idea of a self-portrait does haunt me. It's what I want to do all the time. I keep coming back to it, to record where I am, where this organism is – both in the world and in time."[18]

"To record where I am" seems to be a fundamentally important statement for the artist, as both in his poetry and in his paintings, Jim Dine is concerned with manifesting his own efforts – shaped by personal and micro-social memories, by dramatic emotional energies, wishful dreams and imaginings, by longings and inner forces driving him – to grasp his own path and genuine situation, his authentic self and real place, the personal, but at the same time also social, cultural and intelligible entirety of his being. For this reason, his self-portraits are not simply self-representations, but rather a testament to his struggle to find the self that is always hidden behind various masks and scenes, behind sociocultural settings and "alter ego figures." In his monumental, often demonic, yet at the same time also self-ironic self-portraits, the massive, gigantic form of his head stands before the beholder like an ancient, archaic stele, timeless, immovable and powerful. Within the contours of these self-portraits, he creates a dense, vivid and affecting aura – tormented by inner antagonisms and tensions, sensual and dramatic, obscure and oppressive – from

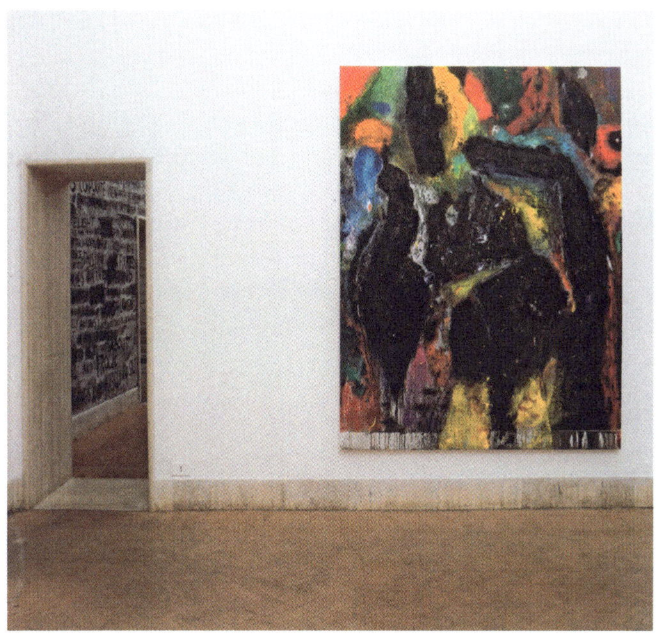

Installation view of the exhibition "Jim Dine. House of Words. The Muse and Seven Black Paintings," Accademia Nazionale di San Luca, Rome, 2017-2018

numerous small, vivid formations, unrestricted movements, uncontrollable and picturesque blends, from incomprehensible conjunctions of body parts and facial elements, and from figures that suggest spatial situations. The overall aura appears as a visual reality that is both encyclopedically universal and specifically singular, manifesting Jim Dine's engagement with existential complexity.

"To record where I am" is also an extremely important statement, because in Jim Dine's poetry, metaphorical, imaginary voyages are given absolutely fundamental significance – the representation of the desire to move somewhere, or to reach a place of great importance to him, a symbolically significant place, or to arrive, to be at home somewhere. It is hard and painful, dramatic and essential to find a true, genuine and authentic place, to find a spiritual community, and thus to find oneself. The sincerity and the drama of this hard path can be heard in his poems. Like his poems, his self-portraits also convey precisely this dramatic note with their diabolical, compulsive and repetitive tone, betraying a dark obsession, extremely sensual, self-destructive and self-tormenting, but also self-ironic, and always monumental and irresistible. The artist's face or head is depicted as a wild terrain of furiously raging, psychological energies, of conflicting, excessive and emotional forces. Identification with the self, the quest to grasp and understand oneself, to localize oneself somewhere, to give the self a "home" – a home "in the world and in time," as Jim Dine puts it – fills this dramatic encounter with the self with emotion and an inner flame.

This very personal statement, "to record where I am," also reveals further important aspects to us – references and historical moments that have great meaning in Jim Dine's work as an artist. The question of "where I am," which Jim Dine has posed as an old artist with many experiences and life events, with an enormous oeuvre behind him, latently refers to the temporal and spatial localization of the artist's cultural, linguistic, anthropological and psychological position. The simple word "where" asks for many things: it asks for the place, thus in the metaphorical sense for the spiritual and cultural context, for the country, home, language and culture in every aspect; but it also asks for the position in time, thus in the metaphorical sense for the historical, cultural, intellectual and mythological era in which the artist – the wanderer – resides.

In the figure of the wanderer, the actual, concrete and real person of the artist Jim Dine integrates the shared moments, experiences and memories of a larger community in which his personal history, his cultural preferences and his existential orientation are rooted, from the Jewish peasants in the Baltics to his grandfather, an Ohio craftsman, and to his parents and family, various uncles who earned their living with manual labor. From his rural childhood to his small-town youth, in the Jewish lower middle-class, where life was defined by craftsmanship and working on tangible things, on materials and real, everyday, simple problems, and to the first years of his education, with various experiences in different genres of art, Jim Dine's immediate environment was always connected to handcraft. Many of his drawings, paintings and sculptures often seem like something of a monument to this world of tools in workshops or farmhouses, closely stacked and in a state of organic disorder that embodies the intensity of an emotionally defined, auratic atmosphere rather than any material reality. This painted atmosphere is a potential answer to the question of "where I am;" in his paintings, the artist creates his home.

The question, then, also involves the potential alternative of cultural nomadism, that is, the possibility that the artist may not automatically and unconditionally, fatalistically and quasi unproblematically consider and value his "given" era as his natural and, in particular, his one and only home, but rather may go wandering in other cultures, other eras, other historical and cultural contexts. Of course, he will do so with the clear consciousness of the wanderer, who is well aware of the fact that he is "only" a wanderer, that his sojourn in different eras, various realms of selected cultures and diverse contexts of artistic methodology is "only" temporary and metaphorical, as he seeks to find authentic and relevant material for his own creative and intellectual endeavors. Jim Dine's never hidden connection to painterly tradition can be understood as a sign of such sovereignty and spiritual independence of any form of intellectual compulsion to constantly produce something "new," to always be "original," "current" and "contemporary," to compulsively and exclusively represent and reflect the newest, freshest and latest novelties. The debate about "the new" and its value in contemporary art, described by Harold Rosenberg in the chapter entitled "The New as Value" of his great book *The Anxious Object*, very clearly illuminates the issue of understanding each iteration of "the new." The mechanical, quasi-automatic identification of "the new" as "value" – imposed by a group in the New York art scene at the time – can be interpreted as a typical phenomenon of the historical and cultural era of the early 1960s.[19]

We, in the here and now, can see Jim Dine's clear, deliberate resistance as a young artist – who had been a celebrated star of the early exhibition and performance scene himself, had participated in all significant exhibitions of the new Pop Art in New York, and had been presented as an artist in the exhibition "The New Realists" at the Sidney Janis Gallery – against this naïve, unconditional worship of "the new," and against the immediate and automatic equation of "the new" (meaning the representation of the new world of objects of urban everyday life in works of art) with aesthetic "value." In numerous interviews and discussions, Jim Dine stressed that he would not be limited by such worship of "the new," that he would present his work in the overall, historical tradition of painting. Lucy R. Lippard has even called Jim Dine "non-Pop," highlighting his resistance to the mainstream of new Pop Culture: "A third non-Pop parodistic current is represented by a single artist: Jim Dine. And although he is frequently included in the Pop rosters, his every work and statement shows him to be worlds apart from that tough iconoclasm and formal emphasis. The complexities of Dine's highly personal and ultimately destructive art are controversial."[20] In addition to the steadily repeated claim that Jim Dine's oeuvre actually does not belong to the mainstream of Pop Art, Lucy R. Lippard's assessment appears of particular significance here: namely the description of Jim Dine's art as actually "destructive" and "controversial."

In this context, in the cultural and historical era of early Pop Art and the various forms of so-called New Realism and Neo-Dada in Europe and the United States, when youthful, fresh and optimistic rebellion against all hierarchy and authority unfolded angrily, radically and subversively – against everything that the young generation saw as old, traditional or established, as recognized, conventional and officially respected, or simply as pathos-laden, academic, formalistic and old-fashioned – a subtle, complex artistic position such as Jim Dine's could be considered "destructive" and "controversial," as the artist did not emphasize a renewal of artistic expression, nor "the new" as such (as in a renewed technique or form of representation, or the new world of objects manifested in the work of art) as an absolute, indisputable and self-evident aesthetic value. In contrast, Jim Dine advocated the authenticity of the message of art, the poetic complexity of works of art, and the emotional perfection of artistic creation. In this, the substance of his narrative was formed by cultural and historical references, micro-social experiences, and allusions to memories and events that connected the artist's present to the past of his descent, his origins and his personal history. The novelties of his present and the new experiences of the current, contemporary situation are elements of this narrative; there is

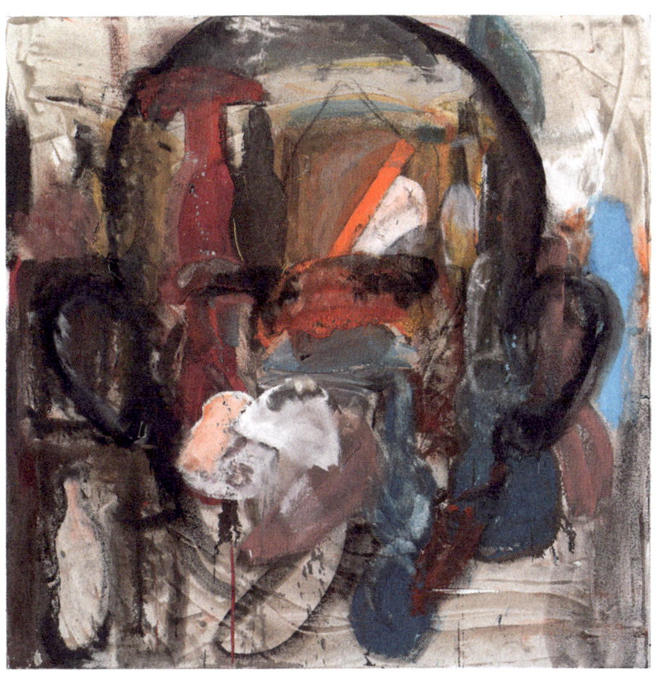

Jim Dine
Other Poems, 2017
Acrylic and sand on linen, 150 x 150 cm
Courtesy Galerie Templon, Paris and Bruxelles

no rigid divide between past and present, between personal and micro-social experiences, between immediate realities and intelligible conventions, imaginings and reflections.

In fact, he was not concerned with tradition, with preserving old techniques of painting and models of configuration and composition, especially not in the formal sense, but rather with sovereignty and emotionality, with an artistic, poetic perspective on the material realities of the new, urban consumer society, and with a free, individual painterly interpretation of the objects of contemporary everyday life. While many New York artists, critics, collectors and journalists spoke of the necessity of representing "the new" in metropolitan life, of unconditional recognition for the presence of material realities in a consumer world, and in particular of the equation of "the

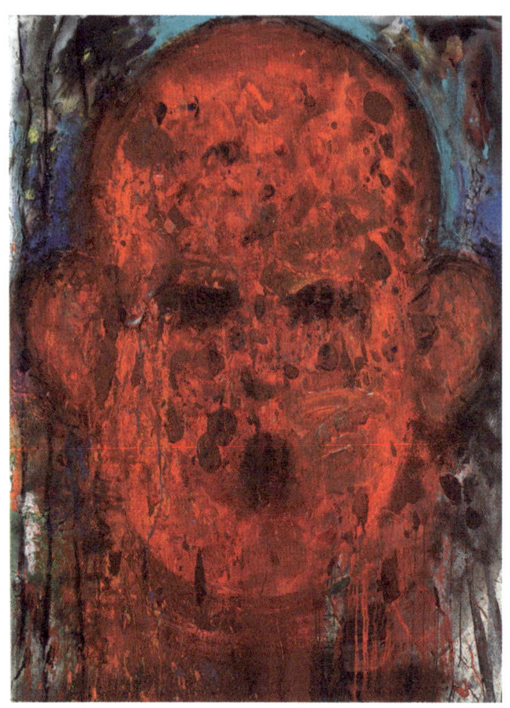

Jim Dine
Red Poet Singing "My puzzled mind", 2017
Oil, acrylic and sand on linen, 170 x 126 cm
Courtesy Galerie Templon, Paris and Bruxelles

new" with artistic value, Jim Dine defended a conception of value that did not detach itself from the history of art. He saw no antagonism between tradition and the present, between a connection to old art and the representation of new realities. Jim Dine considered the objects of contemporary everyday life in the context of their anthropological, cultural, historical and micro-social embeddedness, in their auratic, intelligible and evocative complexity of meaning, as embodiments of a very specific, complex and personal narrative.

In our contemporary view of history and aesthetics, the artist has – historically – also been given this option: he can chose his mental place in the stream of history in every way; he can build the foundation of his work from different cultural elements, and fundamentally determine the appropriate, adequate context of his practice, and a suitable framework for his way of thinking and his techniques, from his artistic preferences and his spiritual orientations. This also implies a sort of cultural nomadism, or a kind of independence of the constraints of time, of the compulsion to espouse what is "new" and "contemporary," especially as the inherently fluid category of "contemporary" never had a self-sufficient definition, but rather followed ostensible conventions within a limited group, always shaped by current fashions and expectations. Although there is little significance to it in this context, and it has been sufficiently discussed before, it should nonetheless be stressed that this sort of cultural nomadism – this sovereign, free determination of the artist's position; this profound connection to old cultural traditions; this generous, romantic independence of a given, limited, specific period in history; this courageous freedom of the dubious imperative to be "new," "contemporary" and "current;" the will to detach oneself and give oneself a chance to work with all possible techniques, even with references to old, classical art and visual narratives of earlier eras – all this set Jim Dine apart from the majority of artists of the Pop Art scene in New York from the very beginning.

What appears more significant here, though, is that the artist defines his fundamental, visual narrative in a continuous process of searching for the place and time of his existence, in the search for his home. This aesthetic search for a home – which is also, in the broader sense, a universal human search for a spiritual home – is no doubt rooted in the artist's entire life history, in the complexity of his origin in the historical and metaphorical sense. As with everyone, his origin inevitably and essentially involves much that is communal, cultural, historical and ethnographic, historically concretizing the complexity of self. It is precisely this concreteness – always individual and bound to its context, never interchangeable – that is given a communal, metaphorical meaning through the artist's work, in which the concrete, individual, singular and unique reality of life, the specific continuum of life, is transformed into a metaphorical narrative.

"Jim Dine's art is substantially autobiographical. He explores family events, things from his studio and the household. To a great extent, he takes into account artistic traditions, which he seeks to renew in a way appropriate to his painting. Like Jasper Johns, he cultivates a culture of painting that appears in a new light in his work to the extent that he does not adopt it conventionally, but rather deliberately sets it in a new context," wrote Rolf-Gunter Dienst;[21] to us, the autobiographical determination appears to be the decisive element in Jim Dine's specific narrative. His poems, his writings, but also his numerous interviews speak directly or indirectly of members of his family, in the far-away countries from which they came, and out of the olden times from which they hail us, making them participants in the poetic narrative of Jim Dine's art.

The evocative allusions to impermanence and temporality, to micro-social and local meaning, to the stream of time and events into which each person was thrown, and the poetic connection between the temporal and spatial frames of life invigorated by memories, create a dense, extremely complex, auratic sphere in which the singular, yet metaphorical narrative of the painting unfolds. The tools of a rural or small-town environment, through which people, situations, conditions of life and events of the past are called to mind, populate this visual universe with subtle, latent, both personal and communal narratives.

Jim Dine supplies a beautiful example of this sensitive, subtle merging of specifically experienced, personal moments, subjective emotions, and micro-social, cultural, learned and adopted ideas that always forms the basis of his narrative, when he remembers the creation of an early woodcut: "Then I saw Paul Sachs' book. I saw the German expressionist woodcuts. I saw Kirchner. I saw Nolde. I saw Max Beckmann's etchings. I was shocked by them, and so I went into my grandpa's basement, in our basement where I lived, and I began to carve things on old pieces of wood he had down there, or a top of a table. And I remember the first print I made, I think, was of a rabbi, an old-fashioned shtetl rabbi. Now I don't know where I got this idea from. I didn't come from a religious house. But it was more likely it was from photographs my grandpa had of his father, who always wore a yarmulke, a prayer cap, because the picture sort of looked like my grandpa. So it must have been 'Grandpa Cohen,' as we called him. I never knew him."[22]

Jim Dine's beautiful description of the background to his work shows very vividly how the various mental and emotional elements, his specific, personal situation at the time, the intelligible, mental and conventional elements, and the memories and stories of his family, and – through them – of his cultural, religious micro-community codetermined the content and emotionally influenced his creation of the print. Although, as he says, he never knew his great-grandfather; although he had not had a religious upbringing and had had no intention of making a picture of a rabbi, the result was a visual merging of all these narratives, which have determined the complexity of Jim Dine's concrete, personal life experiences and thus his thinking as an artist. For us, it is significant because it also shows very clearly that Jim Dine's poetic, overall narrative is very much open to specific, personal, micro-historical, sociocultural and anthropological realities, where the intensity of each experience – often connected with imaginative, fictional, literary and meditative elements – invalidates and eliminates any restriction of content or constraint of form. He acts in complete freedom; he does not allow any formalistic considerations to constrain him; he adheres neither to structural rules nor to thematic lines: in each case, the visual dramaturgy of his overall narrative determines the visual and sculptural formation.

That is why Jim Dine's oeuvre – his literary works and his performance art just as much as his visual and sculptural work – exhibits an unusual formal openness and diversity. His visual narrative, language and dramaturgy have been variously determined not only by the spiritual orientation of his different creative periods, but also by the diverse historical, philosophical and ethical challenges to which he has sought authentic answers in his choice of themes and styles. It seems that this great and, in some ways, lonely master lives in constant emotional and intellectual intensity, seeking to relate all of human experience to himself, with all its dramatic events and extremes, all its painful questions and doubts, and the unbearable weight of memory, in order to create authentic metaphors in which the entirety of our life and our fate is manifested. Perhaps it is this heroism – or this obsession –

that fills his oeuvre with dramatic, often dark melancholia, which he then relativizes with his irony and his almost diabolical, self-tormenting sense of humor.
This psychological, emotional and intellectual complexity is manifest in particularly obvious and compelling ways in the extremely suggestive, monumental self-portraits he has created in recent years. Their dramatic intensity and rich, obsessive density is sometimes reminiscent of the German Expressionists, and other times of American Abstract Expressionism, though without seeking to revive the aesthetics of those times. What appears on these powerful, incredibly intense, enigmatic and irrational paintings is a dense, poetic yet drastic, almost barbaric aura, torn by inner tensions and massive antagonisms, wounded by brutality, battles and wars, yet nonetheless completely coherent and rich, replete with diverse micro-events, references, associations and imaginings, and containing a permanent, inner process of self-interrogation and self-searching that is conflicted, contradictory, painful and disconcerting. When he recently asserted in a conversation that "everything I do is self-portraiture,"[23] he thus summarized the significance of his self-portraits for his artistic vision and, more generally, the significance of artistic work for his life: grasping the self, in its varied determinations, its diverse cultural contexts, and its multiplicity of specific sociocultural, ethnic, linguistic and religious communities – in its singular and, at the same time, paradigmatic nature.

Referring to Rembrandt's self-portraits, Jim Dine writes about his actual, ultimate motivation to paint self-portraits: "He is my favorite self-portraitist. I thought he found his face infinitely as interesting as I find mine. I'm not talking personality-wise, I mean, you know, what you see in the mirror every morning, the many disguises that the visage has. And it's yours."[24] This is the mystery, the enigma or, to the contrary, the only truth, the only reality: one's own face, which holds the true, specific and unique history of one's own self. The face that appears in the mirror is the reality of one's self. It is what the artist seeks to grasp, to comprehend, to understand and to bear. That is his drama.

To grasp his self, the artist creates "alter ego figures" that actually interpret the various roles of his self. Like a sorcerer's apprentice of painting, Jim Dine conjures up diverse characters and figures, from family members to Pinocchio and from self-portraits to ape-people, that encounter his own self-portraits and appear together, hand in hand, on the fictional, imaginary stage of his visual stories. He approaches his self with self-irony and self-interrogation, with irresistible curiosity, but also with destabilizing anxiety.

Jim Dine's visual narrative comprises the most personal, intimate and subjective moments, as well as poetic, metaphorical elements and literary, narrational and anecdotal accounts, but also dramatic, emotionally explosive and eccentric events, all as part of his constant search for an appropriate, authentic position in time and place in the world, for an emotional and spiritual home. In this complex, dense narrative that is theatrically and epically staged, and equal parts touching, elemental and essential, personal memories, specific experiences and real events are merged with imaginative, intelligible and fictional elements that the artist did not directly experience himself, but that he passes on and vividly internalizes in his spiritual world through accounts, stories, micro-social experiences and collective memories. Scenes from his grandfather's rural living conditions, the presence of tools and various implements used in agricultural labor – organically determined by their use for work, yet at the same time admired as objects of desire and hung in clear order on the wall – profoundly influenced his view of art and his conception of the poetic potential of visual representation.

From the very beginning, the omnipresent tools – sometimes old, almost archaic objects that were used for manual labor and constant work with materials, for the process of producing or repairing various things – induced a sort of romanticization of the material world in his oeuvre, though this led in a different direction than with many artists of the Pop Culture of the time: in Jim Dine's oeuvre, the objects are integrated into a heavy, dark atmosphere marked by poverty and suffering, or into a peculiar, theatrical mood marked by self-irony and parody, grotesquerie and cabaret. Through this, a deeply emotional, multilayered, poetic yet also ironic aura emerges in his oeuvre, relating all elements of this dense, emotional, ambivalent and complex universe very closely to the person of the artist, even if they do not directly represent the material environment of his life.

Jim Dine's complex, poetic visual narrative unfolds on an enormous, wide and unimaginably dense field of metaphorical evocations that generate and maintain a continuous, vivid, perceptible and emotional connection between memory and everyday reality, between private, personal and singular elements on the one hand, and micro-social, cultural and historical, collective and culturally intelligible elements on the other hand. In this sense, it can be said that Jim Dine's oeuvre – his poetry and his visual poetry – involves essential, fundamental anthropological realities that are undeniable and intelligible, that are always connected to his concrete life, his personal life experiences, his visions and his memory. A latent, subtle irony – or self-irony – blends with the profound, romantic emotions that shape the entire complexity and continuum of life.

This visual narrative, which is romantic, dramatic and self-referential yet also communal, manifests in a vehemently expressive, subversively sensual and vivid way, posing the eternal question of an authentic place and an appropriate time, of a potential language, a sovereign semiotic system and symbol structure, in the form of a continuous voyage through time and space, through history and the world, the individual and the communal, the past and the present. As he expressed it so radically in his poem *Nantes* that interweaves his passionate, diverse experiences, impressions, memories and feelings: "I am happy to be a prisoner of my ageless emotions."[25]

(2017)

1. Harold Rosenberg: *The Anxious Object – Art Today and Its Audience. A Mentor Book*, The New American Library, New York and Toronto 1964, 1966, 1969, p. 185.
2. Jim Dine in a conversation with Bruce Glaser about Pop Art, with the participation of Robert Indiana and James Rosenquist, in: *1964. Quoted by Lucy R. Lippard: Pop Art*, Thames and Hudson, London 1966, p. 106.
3. Lucy R. Lippard: *Pop Art*, Thames and Hudson, London 1966, p. 9.
4. Many authors underline the great difference between the various European "Neo-realist" and "Neo-Dada" movements, and Pop Art in the United States, arguing that the European Pop Art formations and the different "Neo-realisms" had a much more radical, ideological orientation and protested against the capitalist consumer world much more consistently than the American artists. Some European artists, such as Erró and Fromanger, spoke out directly against the Vietnam War or the Pinochet dictatorship in their works; other artists attacked

the capitalist cult of consumerism, though always in ways mingled with a kind of euphoria for the (naïvely viewed) modern era. Lucy R. Lippard has exhaustively explored the various politically motivated, anti-capitalist, critical and destructive movements within Pop Art or at its margins, such as the March Gallery group, or Boris Lurie and Sam Goodman's "NO!art," and the "Doom" artists around the Gallery Gertrude Stein. In this regard, it should be stated that these movements and groups, determined by radical, critical ideologies, were actually perceived by contemporary audiences under the general category of Pop Culture or Pop Art even at the time of their emergence. Rolf-Gunter Dienst, for instance, spoke of a sort of indifference: "Here, with most American artists of this style (i.e. Pop Art – L.H.), an indifferent mix of object fetishism and idolization (Marilyn Monroe) appears, which is coupled with a desire for visual agitation that does not go beyond the realm of aesthetics." (In: Rolf-Gunter Dienst: *Pop Art – Eine kritische Information*, Limes Verlag, Wiesbaden 1965, p. 16).

5. Ágnes Berecz: *Close Encounters: On Pierre Restany and Nouveau Réalisme*, in: *New Realisms: 1957-1962. Object Strategies Between Readymade and Spectacle*, Julia Robinson (ed.), Museo Nacional Centro de Arte Reina Sofia, Madrid – The MIT Press, Cambridge, MA/London 2010, p. 57.

6. Rolf-Gunter Dienst: op. cit., p. 16.

7. Alice Goldfarb Marquis: *The Pop Revolution – The People Who Radically Transformed the Art World*, Tate Publishing, MFA Publications, Museum of Fine Arts, Boston 2010, p. 141.

8. Ibid., p. 137.

9. Lawrence Alloway: *The Development of British Pop*, in: Lucy R. Lippard: *Pop Art*, Thames and Hudson, London 1966, p. 31.

10. Rolf-Gunter Dienst: op. cit., p. 15.

11. Lucy R. Lippard: *Pop Art*, Thames and Hudson, London 1966, p. 27.

12. Jim Dine: *A Printmaker's Document*, Steidl, Göppingen 2013, p. 14.

13. Lucy R. Lippard: op. cit. , p. 106.

14. Rolf-Gunter Dienst: op. cit., p. 41.

15. Jim Dine: op. cit., p. 228.

16. Lucy R. Lippard quotes Jim Dine's statement in an interview with Bruce Glaser in 1964. See: Lucy R. Lippard: op. cit., p. 106.

17. Alice Goldfarb Marquis: op. cit., p. 44.

18. Jim Dine in an interview with Michael Rooks, in: *Jim Dine – Looking at the Present*, exhibition catalogue, Richard Gray Gallery, April-June 2017, Chicago and New York 2017, p. 6.

19. Harold Rosenberg described the debate about "the new" in contemporary art and its connection to the formation of value, or the consideration of "the new" as an absolute value. In the 20th chapter of his famous book *The Anxious Object – Art Today and Its Audience*, Rosenberg analyzed the standpoint of the director of the Solomon R. Guggenheim Museum at the time, Thomas M. Messer, who – after several important exhibitions of the young Pop Artists – had devoted a significant exhibition at his museum to the new movement in art. The debate about "the new" in art, and about its value, extended far beyond the circles of museums and critics, as it actually dealt with fundamental questions of determining the value of the new methods, which did not exhibit any traditional, formal principles. See: Harold Rosenberg: *The Anxious Object – Art Today and Its Audience. A Mentor Book*, The New American Library, New York and Toronto, 1964, 1966, 1969, p. 184.

20. Lucy R. Lippard: op. cit., p. 105.

21. Rolf-Gunter Dienst: op. cit., p. 39.

22. Jim Dine: op. cit., p. 7.

23. Jim Dine in an interview with Michael Rooks, in: *Jim Dine – Looking at the Present*, op. cit., p. 7.

24. Jim Dine: op. cit., p. 94.

25. Jim Dine: *Nantes*, Edition Joca Seria, Nantes 2017, p. 22.

LÓRÁND HEGYI

Biography

Lóránd Hegyi was born in Budapest where he studied history, art history and aesthetics. During the 1980s he dedicated himself to curating contemporary art exhibitions while writing art historical and theoretical texts about Modernism and Post-Modernism. In 1982 he published the book *New Sensibility – Change of Paradigm in Contemporary Art* (Budapest: Magvetö). In 1986 he published the book *Avant-Garde and Trans-Avant-Garde – Periods of Modern Art* (Budapest: Magvetö). Shortly after the fall of the Berlin Wall, he was invited to Austria, where from 1990 to 2001 he was director of the Ludwig Museum Vienna. There he created a major collection of central and eastern European art. In 1999 he curated the exhibition "50 Years of Art in Central Europe 1949-1999" (Vienna, Budapest, Southampton), and the show "La Casa, il Corpo, il Cuore – Construction of Identities" (Vienna, Prague). In 2001 he opened the new contemporary art museum MUMOK, Vienna. In 2003 he was the art director of the Valencia Biennale, where he curated the exhibition "Solares." From 2002 to 2006 he was art director of PAN, Naples. From 2003 to 2016 he was director of the Museum of Modern Art of Saint-Étienne. In 2004, he published the book *The Courage to be Alone – Re-inventing Narratives in Contemporary Art* (Milan: Edizioni Charta). In 2005 he curated the exhibition "The Giving Person" in PAN, Naples. In 2008 he published the book *Fragilità della narrativa* (Milan: Skira); in the same year he curated the show "Sensitive Systems – Lee Ufan, Roman Opalka, Giuseppe Penone, Günther Uecker" in Seoul and the show "The Bearable Lightness of Being – The Metaphor of Space" at the Venice Biennial of Architecture. In 2008 he was one of the art directors of the Poznan Biennial where he curated the show "Sentimental Journey." In 2009 he curated the show "Essential Experiences" in Palermo. In 2010 he published the book *Arte in centro Europa – Malinconia, Fluidità, Sovversività* (Cinisello Balsamo: Silvana Editoriale); in the same year he curated the show "Isole mai trovate" (Genoa, Thessaloniki, Saint-Étienne). In 2012 he curated the show "Speaking Artists" in Busan. Also in 2012 he published the book *Contemporary Art on Show* (Cinisello Balsamo: Silvana Editoriale). In 2015 he published the book *Roman Opalka's Essentiality* (Turin: Nino Aragno Editore). In 2016 he curated the exhibition "Intriguing Uncertainties" (Saint-Étienne) and the show "Challenging Beauty – Italian Art After the 60s" (Beijing). In the same year he published the book *Significanti incertezze – Saggio sul disegno contemporaneo* (Turin: Hapax Editore). In 2017 he curated the shows "Anish Kapoor – My Red Homeland" (Saint-Étienne) and "The Artist's Voice" (Singapore).

In 2018 he curated the show "Improbabilities. Uncertainties" (Bruselles). In 2009 he was decorated with the Légion d'Honneur by France.

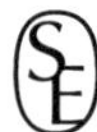

Silvana Editoriale

Direction
Dario Cimorelli

Art Director
Giacomo Merli

Editorial Coordinator
Sergio Di Stefano

Copy Editor
Clia Menici

Layout
Beppe Re Fraschini

Production Coordinator
Antonio Micelli

Editorial Assistant
Ondina Granato

Photo Editor
Alessandra Olivari, Silvia Sala

Press Office
Lidia Masolini, press@silvanaeditoriale.it

Silvana Editoriale S.p.A.
via dei Lavoratori, 78
20092 Cinisello Balsamo, Milan
tel. 02 453 951 01
fax 02 453 951 51
www.silvanaeditoriale.it

Reproductions, printing and binding in Italy
Printed by Artelito, Castelraimondo (Mc)
December 2018

Cover
Michelangelo
Pistoletto
*Il dono di Mercurio
allo specchio*,
detail, 1971

Translation
Alexander Žigo
Judith Wolfframm